LOW-CARB
COOK BOOK

LOW-CARB
COOK BOOK

k

Published by
Kandour Ltd
1-3 Colebrooke Place
London N1 8HZ

This edition published 2005

This edition printed in 2005 for
Bookmart Ltd
Registered Number 2372865
Trading As Bookmart Ltd
Blaby Road
Wigston
Leicester
LE18 4SE

Title: Low Carb Cook Book

Editorial and design management: Metro Media
Author: Victoria Worsley
Design/layout: Lee Coventry
Original design concept: Christine Fent
Photography: photos.com

Printed and bound in India

ISBN 1-904756-33-6

CONTENTS

INTRODUCTION

Made famous by celebrity devotees and endless magazine spreads, low-carb diets have become a well-recognised way of losing weight and improving your health. It is important to remember that low-carb does not mean no-carb. Carbohydrates are an essential component of our overall health, and they should never be entirely omitted from your diet.

However, when following any diet, it can be confusing trying to figure out what you can and cannot eat. This recipe book presents a wide variety of meals that all conform to one thing – they are low-carb and, with proper monitoring, should fit well into a low-carb diet.

From soups and salads to desserts and dips, there are dishes of all sizes and descriptions to choose from, and there is no compromise on taste simply because you are on a diet! Influences range from Europe to Asia and beyond.

So, whether you are strictly following a low-carb diet, or you are cooking for someone who is, or you just want a tasty snack without the guilt-trip, then this is the place to be!

SOUPS

Great as a starter, a snack or a light lunch, soup is a guaranteed family favourite, and also a great pick-me-up if you are feeling low or under the weather. This collection of soup recipes gives you a wide choice of low-carb classics such as tomato soup, chicken soup and minestrone. However, if you're feeling in the mood for something more unusual then why not try Pear and Parsnip soup, or Fennel and Garlic? The essential kitchen item for most of the recipes in this section is a blender or food processor, however you can also press ingredients through a sieve instead, although this process will take a lot longer.

CHICKEN SOUP

Serves 8

INGREDIENTS

3 onions
3 carrots
3 celery stalks
1 large chicken, quartered and skin removed
6 garlic cloves
4 bay leaves
1 tbsp chicken stock powder
4 tbsp chopped fresh parsley
Salt and pepper

Quarter one of each of the vegetables and place in a large saucepan with the chicken, garlic and bay leaves. Cover with water and bring to the boil, then reduce the heat and simmer for 1 hour.

Lift the chicken pieces out of the pan with a slotted spoon and allow to cool. Remove the vegetables and garlic and reserve. Discard the bay leaves. Pull the chicken off the bones and chop it into bite-sized pieces. Set aside.

Skim away any fat from the surface of the stock, then return the chicken bones to the pan. Add about 500ml/16fl oz water, bring to the boil, cover and simmer for 1 hour. Strain the stock through a sieve and return the liquid to the pan.

Put the reserved cooked vegetables into a blender or food processor with a spoonful of the liquid and blend until smooth, then return to the pan.

Finely chop the remaining vegetables and add them to the stock. Add the stock powder and cook for 20 minutes.

Add the chicken and parsley, season well and heat through. Serve hot.

ASPARAGUS SOUP

Serves 4

INGREDIENTS
15g/1/2oz butter
1 celery stalk, chopped
1 onion, chopped
600ml/1pt chicken stock
16 asparagus spears, chopped
125ml/4fl oz double cream
11/2 tbsp snipped fresh chives
Salt and pepper

Heat the butter in a large saucepan. Add the celery and onion
and fry for 5 minutes, or until the onion is soft. Add the stock and
asparagus and bring to the boil. Then reduce the heat and
simmer for 30 minutes.

Transfer the contents of the pan to a blender or food processor
and purée until smooth. Return the mixture to saucepan. Add the
cream, chives and seasoning. Stir to blend and heat gently,
without boiling, until warmed through, then serve.

PEANUT SOUP

Serves 5

INGREDIENTS
3 tbsp butter
3 celery stalks, finely chopped
1 onion, finely chopped
1.8 litres/3pts chicken stock
275g/10oz smooth peanut butter
Salt and pepper
1 tsp guar gum
500ml/16fl oz double cream
50g/2oz salted peanuts, chopped

Melt the butter in a large saucepan and sauté the celery and onion for 3 minutes. Add the stock, peanut butter and seasoning. Stir well, then bring to the boil. Reduce the heat to low, cover and simmer for 1 hour, stirring occasionally.

About 15 minutes before serving, place 225ml/8fl oz of the soup into a blender or food processor. Add the guar gum and pulse for a few seconds, then whisk it back into the soup.

Stir in the cream and simmer for a further 15 minutes. Serve garnished with the peanuts.

LAKSA

Serves 4

INGREDIENTS
1 tbsp sunflower oil
2 garlic cloves, thinly sliced
1 red chilli, deseeded and sliced
2 lemongrass stalks, chopped
2.5cm/1in piece fresh ginger, grated
1.2 litres/2pts fish stock
350g/12oz large raw prawns, peeled and deveined
1 large carrot, grated
100g/4oz shiitake mushrooms, sliced
2 tsp Thai fish sauce

Heat the oil in a large saucepan over a medium heat, then add the garlic, chilli, lemongrass and ginger and cook for 5 minutes, stirring frequently, then add the stock and bring to the boil. Reduce the heat and simmer for 5 minutes.

Stir in the prawns, carrot and mushrooms. Simmer for a further 5 minutes, until the prawns have turned pink.

Stir in the fish sauce and heat through for a further 1 minute before serving.

PEAR AND PARSNIP SOUP

Serves 6

INGREDIENTS
1 tsp olive oil
200g/7oz Savoy cabbage, sliced
1 leek, sliced
2 pears, peeled and roughly chopped
350g/12oz parsnips, roughly chopped
1.2 litres/2pts chicken stock
Salt and pepper
2 tbsp grated Parmesan cheese

Heat the oil in a large saucepan over a medium heat. Add the
cabbage and leek and cook for 3 minutes, stirring regularly. Add
the pears and parsnips and stir well.

Add the stock and bring to the boil, then reduce the heat and
simmer for 30 minutes. Remove from heat and transfer to a
blender or food processor and purée until smooth. Season with
salt and pepper, and serve sprinkled with Parmesan.

AUBERGINE SOUP

Serves 8

INGREDIENTS
4 aubergines, halved
2 tsp olive oil, plus extra for brushing
Salt and pepper
4 garlic cloves, chopped
1 red onion, chopped
2 tomatoes, chopped
1 tsp hot pepper sauce
1 tbsp tomato ketchup

Preheat the oven to 200°C/400°F/Gas mark 6.

Brush the aubergines with the extra olive oil and season with salt and pepper. Place them on a baking tray and roast them in the oven for 45 minutes, turning occasionally. Remove from the oven and leave to cool.

Scoop out the flesh of the aubergine with a spoon and reserve, discarding the skins.

Add the olive oil to a large frying pan over a medium heat. Add the garlic and onion and cook until tender, stirring frequently. Add the aubergine flesh, tomatoes, pepper sauce and ketchup. Serve at room temperature.

CAULIFLOWER SOUP

Serves 4

INGREDIENTS
25g/1oz butter
75g/3oz onion, diced
75g/3oz celery, diced
1.2 litres/2pts chicken stock
300g/11oz frozen cauliflower florets
1/2 tsp guar gum
125ml/4fl oz double cream
Salt and pepper

Melt the butter in a frying pan over a low heat and sauté the onion and celery for 4 minutes. Transfer to a saucepan, add the stock and cauliflower and simmer until the cauliflower is tender.

Transfer the vegetables to a blender or food processor and then pour in as much of the stock as you can. Add the guar and purée the mixture until smooth.

Pour the mixture back into the saucepan. Stir in the cream and season to taste.

FENNEL AND GARLIC SOUP

Serves 8

INGREDIENTS
15 garlic cloves, peeled
500ml/16fl oz double cream
2 large fennel bulbs
Salt and pepper

Place the garlic and cream in a medium-sized pot and bring to the boil over a medium heat. Lower the heat and gently simmer, covered, for 30 minutes, or until the garlic cloves are very soft.

Trim and clean the fennel by cutting off the stalks and fronds from the bulbs. Cut the bulb in half lengthways and trim out the root. Keep the stalks and bulb portion and discard the fronds and root trimmings.

Cut the fennel into 1cm/¹/₂in pieces. Place in a colander, wash thoroughly and drain well.

Add the fennel and 725ml/1¹/₄pts of water to the garlic mixture. Bring to the boil, then lower the heat, cover and simmer for a further 40 minutes.

Transfer the mixture to a blender or food processor and purée until very smooth – you will have to do this in several batches. Return the puréed mixture to the pot and season to taste. Heat through until the soup has thickened slightly. Serve hot.

MUSHROOM SOUP

Serves 8

INGREDIENTS
1/2 tbsp lard
15g/1/2oz butter
100g/4oz onion, finely chopped
150g/5oz mushrooms, chopped
Salt and pepper
225g/8oz sour cream
2 tbsp double cream

Melt the lard and butter in a large frying pan over a medium heat. Add the onion, mushrooms and seasoning, then sauté for 10 minutes, until the mixture is quite thick.

Pour the vegetables into a fairly large bowl and allow them to cool for about 3 minutes. Stir in the sour cream and cream, mixing well.

Purée in batches in a blender or food processor until smooth. Return to the saucepan and heat through serving.

MULLIGATAWNY

Serves 6

INGREDIENTS
1.8 litres/3pts chicken stock
225g/8oz diced cooked chicken or diced boneless, skinless
    chicken breasts
25g/1oz butter
1 garlic clove, crushed
1 onion, chopped
1 carrot, grated
2 celery stalks, diced
2 tsp curry powder
1/2 dessert apple, finely chopped
Salt and pepper
1/2 tsp dried thyme
Grated zest of 1 lemon
225ml/8fl oz double cream

Put the stock and chicken in a large stockpot and place over a
low heat.

Melt the butter in a frying pan and add the garlic, onion, carrot,
celery and curry powder. Sauté for 4 to 6 minutes, or until the
vegetables are soft, then transfer to the pot.

Add the apple, seasoning, thyme and lemon zest and simmer for
30 minutes. Stir in the cream just before serving.

CHUNKY VEGETABLE SOUP

Serves 8

INGREDIENTS
1 tbsp olive oil
1 onion, finely chopped
4 rashers lean back bacon, fat removed, cut into
    2.5cm/1in squares
2 carrots, thinly sliced
2 celery stalks, finely chopped
1/2 Chinese cabbage, sliced
2 courgettes, thinly sliced
1.2 litres/2pts chicken stock
2 garlic cloves, crushed
3 bay leaves
400g/14oz tinned chopped tomatoes
Salt and pepper
50g/2oz Parmesan cheese, grated

Heat the oil in a large saucepan over a medium heat. Add the
onion and bacon. Cook for 3 minutes, or until the onion is soft.

Add the carrots, celery, cabbage and courgettes to the pan and
gently cook, stirring, for 5 minutes. Add the stock, garlic, bay
leaves and tomato and bring to the boil, then reduce the heat and
simmer, covered, for 1 hour. Season to taste and remove the bay
leaves. Sprinkle with Parmesan to serve.

TOMATO SOUP

Serves 4

INGREDIENTS
2 garlic cloves, crushed
1 onion, finely chopped
1 tbsp water
725ml/1¼pt vegetable stock
500ml/16fl oz tomato juice
1 sweet potato, peeled and diced
12 tomatoes, peeled
25g/1oz fresh parsley, finely chopped
25g/1oz fresh basil, finely chopped
1 tbsp fresh rosemary, finely chopped
Salt and pepper

Heat a large saucepan, and add the garlic and onion with the water and sauté for 3 minutes, or until the onion is soft.

Add the stock, tomato juice, sweet potato, tomatoes, herbs and seasoning. Bring to the boil, then reduce the heat and simmer 30 minutes or until the sweet potato is soft.

Transfer the contents of the pan to a blender or food processor and blend until smooth. Return to the pan and reheat before serving.

OLIVE SOUP

Serves 6

INGREDIENTS
1.2 litres/2pts chicken stock
$1/2$ tsp guar gum
100g/4oz black olives, stoned and finely chopped
225ml/8fl oz double cream
75ml/3fl oz dry sherry
Salt and pepper

Put 125ml/4fl oz chicken stock in a blender or food processor
with the guar gum and blend for a few seconds. Pour into a
saucepan and add the remaining stock and the olives.

Heat until simmering, then whisk in the cream. Bring back to a
simmer, stir in the sherry and season to taste before serving.

CHILLED FENNEL SOUP

Serves 6

INGREDIENTS
1 tbsp sunflower oil
450g/1lb fennel bulbs, fronds removed, bulb coarsely chopped
1 onion, chopped
725ml/1$1/4$pts chicken stock
150ml/$1/4$pt sour cream
Salt and pepper

Heat the oil in a large saucepan over a medium heat, then add
the fennel and onion. Cover and simmer for 10 minutes, stirring
occasionally.

Add the stock to the pan and bring to the boil, then reduce the
heat and simmer for 20 minutes.

Transfer to a blender or food processor and process until smooth. Place in a bowl and leave to chill in the refrigerator for at least 3 hours.

When thoroughly chilled, whisk in the sour cream and adjust the seasoning to taste before serving.

TOMATO AND APPLE SOUP

Serves 4

INGREDIENTS
100g/4oz onions, well chopped
50g/2oz butter
200g/7oz tomatoes, chopped
150g/5oz cooking apples, chopped
150ml/¼pt red wine
Salt and pepper
600ml/1pt chicken stock
1 dessert apple, grated

Cook the onions slowly in the butter for 10 minutes. Add the tomatoes, apples and wine and season to taste. Cover and simmer gently for 1 hour.

Purée the contents of the pan in a blender or food processor and then add the stock and reheat, stirring well. Serve hot, sprinkled with the dessert apple.

ONION AND PARSNIP SOUP

Serves 4

INGREDIENTS
1 onion, diced
2 parsnips, diced
1 tbsp olive oil
1/2 tsp garam masala
1/2 tsp curry powder
Salt and pepper
1.2 litres/2pts vegetable stock
2 tbsp chopped walnuts

Sweat the onions and parsnips in the olive oil until they begin to
brown, then add the garam masala, curry powder and seasoning
and cook, stirring occasionally, for a further 2 minutes.
Add the stock and cook, covered, for 15 minutes.

Transfer the soup in batches to a blender or food processor and
pulse until smooth. Reheat, without boiling, and serve topped
with the walnuts.

PARSLEY AND CHICKPEA SOUP

Serves 6

INGREDIENTS
300g/11oz chickpeas, soaked overnight
1 onion, chopped
3 garlic cloves
50g/2oz parsley
2 tbsp olive oil
1.2 litres/2pts vegetable stock
Salt and pepper
Grated zest and juice of 1/2 lemon

Drain the chickpeas and rinse well. Put them in a saucepan and cover with water, then bring to the boil. Reduce the heat and simmer for 1 1/2 hours, until just tender.

Put the onion, garlic and parsley in a blender or food processor and blend until finely chopped.

Heat the oil in a large saucepan and cook the blended onion mixture until slightly softened. Add the chickpeas and cook gently for 2 minutes.

Add the stock, season well with salt and pepper and bring to the boil. Cover and cook for 20 minutes, or until the chickpeas are really tender.

Allow the soup to cool slightly, then part-purée in a blender or food processor. Pour the soup into a clean pan, add the lemon juice and adjust

SALADS

Salad niçoise, Caesar salad, Waldorf salad – a classic salad is a hit at a dinner party or a barbecue, or taken to work in a lunchbox. Salads generally are a central part of most diets, and can be too often perceived as dull and boring. This section aims to prove just how untrue this is, with a selection of recipes that are healthy and low in carbohydrates, as well as being interesting and full of taste. There are salads with fish and meat, as well as those suited to vegetarians. For an added feel-good factor, why not use organic ingredients whenever you can?

SALAD NIÇOISE

Serves 1

INGREDIENTS
1 tbsp olive oil
1/2 tsp coarse grain mustard
1 tbsp red wine vinegar
1 tbsp sour cream
Salt and pepper
50g/2oz cos lettuce, shredded
200g/7oz canned tuna, drained
1 tomato, thinly sliced
1 tbsp capers
50g/2oz green beans, chopped and steamed
6 black olives, stoned
1 hard-boiled egg, cut into quarters

To make the dressing, blend the oil, mustard, vinegar and sour cream until smooth. Season to taste.

Arrange the lettuce on a plate. Gently toss the tuna, tomato, capers, green beans and olives in the dressing, then pile them on the lettuce. Garnish with the egg to serve.

PRAWN SALAD

Serves 2

INGREDIENTS

50ml/2fl oz mayonnaise
1 tbsp fish seasoning
350g/12oz cooked prawns, cut into 1cm/1/2in pieces
8 celery stalks, finely chopped
Salt and pepper
14 romaine lettuce leaves

Combine the mayonnaise and fish seasoning in a medium-sized mixing bowl. Add the prawns and celery and season to taste. Mix well.

Place the lettuce leaves in a salad bowl and top with the prawn mixture to serve.

GREEK SALAD

Serves 4

INGREDIENTS

200ml/7fl oz extra-virgin olive oil
75ml/3fl oz lemon juice
2 tbsp dried oregano, crushed
1 garlic clove, crushed
Salt and pepper
1 large romaine lettuce
50g/2oz fresh parsley, chopped
1/2 cucumber, sliced
1 green pepper, sliced
1/4 red onion, thinly sliced
12 black olives, stoned
2 tomatoes, cut into wedges
150g/5oz feta cheese, crumbled

Place the oil, lemon juice, oregano, garlic and seasoning in a container with a tight-fitting lid and shake well to make the dressing.

Break the lettuce into bite-sized pieces. Add the parsley, cucumber and green pepper.

Pour on the dressing just before serving and toss well.

Scatter the onions, olives and tomatoes over the top and sprinkle with feta to serve.

RICE SALAD

Serves 4

INGREDIENTS
150g/5oz yellow lentils
150g/5oz basmati rice
300g/11oz cannelloni beans, cooked
4 tomatoes, chopped
1 cucumber, chopped
2 tbsp finely chopped fresh oregano leaves
75g/3oz basil leaves, finely chopped
1 tbsp finely chopped garlic chives
Juice of 1 lemon
1 tbsp plain white vinegar
Salt and pepper

Soak and cook lentils following the packet instructions, then allow to cool.

In a saucepan of salted boiling water, cook the basmati rice, then drain and allow to cool.

Combine the lentils and rice with the beans, tomatoes, cucumber, oregano, basil, garlic chives, lemon juice, vinegar and seasoning in a large mixing bowl, mix well and serve.

BACON AND GOATS' CHEESE SALAD

Serves 2

INGREDIENTS
75ml/3fl oz olive oil
2 tbsp fresh lemon juice
1 tsp Dijon mustard
2 tsp minced fresh dill
Salt and pepper
3 celery stalks, chopped
350g/12oz spinach leaves, washed
6 spring onions, trimmed and chopped
50g/2oz goats' cheese, crumbled
150g/5oz button mushrooms, sliced
4 rashers smoked bacon, cooked and crumbled

Mix together the olive oil, lemon juice, Dijon honey mustard, dill and seasoning to taste in a blender or food processor, and process until smooth.

In mixing bowl, combine the celery, spinach, spring onions, goat cheese, mushrooms and a quarter of the prepared salad dressing. Toss to coat. Place the salad in a large salad bowl and sprinkle with the bacon. Serve the remaining dressing on the side.

MONKFISH SALAD

Serves 4

INGREDIENTS
25g/1oz pine nuts
1 tsp Dijon mustard
3 tbsp olive oil
1 tsp sherry vinegar
1 garlic clove, crushed
Salt and pepper
2 monkfish fillets, about 350g/12oz each, sliced

225g/8oz baby spinach leaves, washed and stalks removed
Salt and pepper

Heat a dry frying pan, add the pine nuts and shake them over a low heat until golden brown. Transfer to a plate and reserve.

To make the dressing, put the mustard, 2 tablespoons olive oil, sherry vinegar and garlic in a small bowl and whisk thoroughly until smooth. Pour into a small saucepan, season to taste and warm through over a low heat.

Heat the remaining oil in a frying pan, then add the monkfish and sauté for about 30 seconds on each side.

Put the spinach leaves in a large bowl and pour the warm salad dressing over. Sprinkle the roasted pine nuts over the top and toss together. Divide the spinach leaves between four serving plates and place the monkfish on top. Serve immediately.

SPINACH SALAD

Serves 2

INGREDIENTS
1 tbsp fresh-squeezed lime juice
4 drops hot chilli oil
1^{1}/$_{2}$ tsp sesame oil
^{1}/$_{8}$ tsp sugar substitute
1 tsp sesame seeds
Salt and pepper
450g/1lb baby spinach leaves
2 tbsp chopped fresh chives
150g/5oz fresh beansprouts

In a small dish, combine the lime juice, chilli oil, sesame oil, sugar substitute, sesame seeds and seasoning.

In a large bowl, combine the spinach, chives and beansprouts. Drizzle the spinach with the dressing and serve immediately.

AVOCADO AND MOZZARELLA SALAD

Serves 1

INGREDIENTS
1/2 avocado, peeled and thinly sliced
75g/3oz Mozzarella cheese, thinly sliced
1 tomato, thinly sliced
1 tbsp lemon juice
1 tbsp pesto sauce
Salt and pepper

Arrange the avocado, Mozzarella and tomato slices on a large plate. Mix together the lemon juice and pesto and drizzle evenly over the top. Season to taste and allow the flavours to blend for 10 minutes before serving.

CUCUMBER SALAD

Serves 8

INGREDIENTS
3 cucumbers, thinly sliced
Salt and pepper
25g/1oz sugar substitute
75ml/3fl oz white wine vinegar
225ml/8fl oz sour cream
1 tsp chopped fresh dill
50g/2oz onion, finely chopped

Put the cucumber in a large bowl and sprinkle with 3 teaspoons salt. Refrigerate for at least 2 hours. Drain off the water, then rinse and drain again.

Dissolve the sugar substitute in the vinegar, whisk in the sour cream, dill and onion, and fold the mixture into the cucumber slices. Season to taste, and serve.

EGG SALAD

Serves 2

INGREDIENTS
75ml/3fl oz mayonnaise
1/2 tsp prepared mustard
1 celery stalk, diced
6 spring onions, sliced
1/2 green pepper, diced
75g/3oz cos lettuce, shredded
4 eggs, hard-boiled and chopped

In a small bowl mix together the mayonnaise and mustard.

In a large salad bowl, toss together the celery, spring onions and green pepper, then stir the dressing through.

Serve salad on a bed of cos lettuce, with the eggs scattered over the top.

CHEESE AND HAM SALAD

Serves 2

INGREDIENTS
1 slice ham, 5mm/¼in thick, sliced into 5cm/2in strips
25g/1oz Swiss cheese, sliced into 5cm/2in strips
3 tbsp finely chopped celery
100g/4oz mushrooms, sliced
2 tbsp finely chopped parsley
1 tsp white wine vinegar
1 tbsp olive oil
1 tsp Dijon mustard
1 tbsp double cream
2 tbsp grated Parmesan cheese
Salt and pepper

Place the ham and cheese into a large mixing bowl along with the celery, mushrooms and parsley.

Combine the vinegar, oil, mustard, cream and cheese in a small mixing bowl and whisk to blend. Adjust the seasoning to taste. Toss the dressing with the ham and cheese mixture to coat evenly and serve immediately.

CAESAR SALAD

Serves 4

INGREDIENTS
2 cos lettuces
125ml/4fl oz olive oil
4 rashers rindless bacon, chopped
12 canned anchovies, chopped, oil from can reserved
100g/4oz Parmesan cheese, grated
4 tbsp sour cream
1 garlic clove, crushed
2 eggs, boiled for 1 minute
1/2 tsp Tabasco sauce
Juice of 1/2 lemon
1/2 tsp mustard powder
Salt and pepper
6 eggs, hard-boiled and halved
Extra shaved Parmesan to garnish

Separate the lettuce leaves and rinse thoroughly, then place in a large salad bowl.

Heat 1 tablespoon olive oil in a frying pan and cook the bacon until crisp. Crumble the bacon into a mixing bowl, add the anchovies and Parmesan and mix well.

In a small bowl combine the remaining olive oil, the sour cream, garlic, anchovy oil, soft-boiled eggs, Tabasco sauce, lemon juice, mustard powder and seasoning, and whisk to combine well. Pour the dressing over the bacon mixture. Pile the mixture on top of the lettuce leaves, then top with the hard-boiled eggs and Parmesan shavings to serve.

SPICY CHICKEN SALAD

Serves 4

INGREDIENTS

1/2 tsp cayenne pepper
1/2 tsp paprika
2 tsp seasoned salt
1/2 tsp dried thyme
1/2 tsp onion powder
1/2 tsp garlic powder
1/2 tsp dried oregano
1/2 tsp ground black pepper
675g/1½lb boneless, skinless chicken breasts
425g/15oz packet mixed baby greens

Mix together the cayenne pepper, paprika, salt, thyme, onion powder, garlic powder, oregano and black pepper in a small bowl to blend. Trim any excess fat off the chicken breasts, then dust each side of the chicken with the seasoning.

Cook each side of the chicken under a hot grill for about 5 minutes, or until cooked through. Serve the warm chicken breasts over the mixed baby greens.

BLT SALAD

Serves 2

INGREDIENTS
10 rashers smoked bacon
1/4 tsp crushed garlic
50ml/2fl oz mayonnaise
1 tbsp lemon juice
1 tbsp snipped chives
1 tbsp water
Salt and pepper
1 red onion, thinly sliced
225g/8oz cherry tomatoes, halved
150g/5oz Cheddar cheese, grated
1 head Romaine lettuce, torn into bite-size pieces

In a frying pan, cook the bacon over a medium heat until crisp. Drain on kitchen paper, then crumble and reserve.

In a small bowl, whisk together the garlic, mayonnaise, lemon juice, chives, water and seasoning. In a large bowl toss together the onion, tomatoes, cheese, lettuce, bacon and enough of the prepared dressing to coat. Serve with any remaining dressing on the side.

CHICKEN AND PEANUT SALAD

Serves 4

INGREDIENTS

2 apples, cored and chopped
1 tbsp lemon juice
100g/4oz baby spinach leaves
300g/11oz grilled chicken breast, chopped
1 tbsp unsalted roasted peanuts
4 tomatoes, chopped
1/2 small cucumber, chopped
2 tbsp balsamic vinegar
Salt and pepper

Put the apple pieces in a large bowl, sprinkle with the lemon juice and toss well to coat. Add the spinach, chicken, peanuts, tomatoes and cucumber.

Pour the vinegar over, season to taste and toss well before serving.

WALDORF SALAD

Serves 4

INGREDIENTS
2 large cooked chicken breasts, chopped
4 celery stalks, chopped
1 dessert apple, skin on, chopped
1/2 cucumber, peeled and chopped
75g/3oz pecans, broken
100g/4oz white grapes, halved
75ml/3fl oz mayonnaise
1 tsp lemon juice
75ml/3fl oz yogurt
1/4 tsp sugar substitute
1/4 tsp ground black pepper
Combine the chicken, celery, apple, cucumber, pecans and grapes
in a large salad bowl.

Mix together the mayonnaise, lemon juice, yogurt, sugar substitute and pepper in a small bowl, then pour it over the salad. Mix
well and serve.

TURKEY AND BROCCOLI SALAD

Serves 1

INGREDIENTS
100g/4oz cooked turkey breast, finely chopped
175g/6oz broccoli, finely chopped
50g/2oz spring onion, finely chopped
50g/2oz green pepper, finely chopped
1 tsp chopped fresh tarragon
1 tbsp mayonnaise
2 tsp lemon juice
1 tsp Dijon mustard
Salt and pepper

Put the turkey, broccoli, spring onion, green pepper and tarragon in a bowl. Add the mayonnaise, lemon juice and mustard and combine evenly.

Season with salt and pepper and serve.

MEAT MAIN COURSES

It is in this section that the worldwide influences become evident, with beef provençal, Chinese beef with broccoli and fajitas among the recipes. Chicken, beef, duck, lamb – they are all here, dressed and presented in a wide variety of styles to suit all tastes. You may find some that are more suitable for informal family meals, while others complete a formal dining menu, and you will have a great time experimenting which one suits which occasion best! All recipes are laid out and presented in a simple style that is easy to follow, no matter what your skill level in the kitchen.

STIR-FRY CHICKEN

Serves 3

INGREDIENTS
25ml/1fl oz soy sauce
50ml/2fl oz dry sherry
1 garlic clove, crushed
2.5cm/1in piece fresh ginger, peeled and grated
1/4 tsp guar gum
50ml/2fl oz rapeseed oil
100g/4oz mangetout, cut in half
150g/5oz mushrooms, sliced
50g/2oz sliced water chestnuts
15 spring onions, chopped
3 boneless, skinless chicken breasts, cut into 1cm/1/2in cubes

Stir together the soy, sherry, garlic and ginger and place in a
blender or food processor, add the guar gum and blend well.

Heat 2 tablespoonfuls of oil in a large frying pan and add the
mangetout, mushrooms, water chestnuts and spring onions to
the pan and stir-fry for about 5 minutes. Remove from the pan
and reserve.

Heat the remaining oil in the pan and add the chicken. Stir-fry
for 5 to 7 minutes, or until there is no pink left.

Return the vegetables to the pan and add the soy sauce mixture.
Toss everything together, cover and simmer for 4 minutes.

BEEF HOTPOT

Serves 4

INGREDIENTS
2 tbsp olive oil
4 celery stalks, chopped
6 shallots, peeled
175g/6oz carrots, chopped
500g/1lb 2oz braising steaks, trimmed and diced
1 tbsp plain wholemeal flour
1 tbsp tomato purée
600ml/1pt beef stock
50g/2oz pearl barley, rinsed
Salt and pepper
500g/1lb 2oz sweet potatoes, peeled and chopped

Preheat the oven to 180°C/350°F/Gas mark 4.

Heat half the oil in a large saucepan over a medium heat, add the celery, shallots and carrots and cook for 2 minutes, stirring frequently. Add the steak and cook, stirring constantly, for 3 minutes.

Add the flour and cook for 2 minutes, stirring constantly. Blend the tomato purée with a little of the stock and stir into the saucepan, then stir in the remaining stock and pearl barley. Bring to the boil, stirring constantly, then reduce the heat and simmer for 5 minutes. Season to taste and transfer to a casserole dish.

Arrange the sweet potato on top and brush with the remaining oil. Bake in the preheated oven for 2¹/₂ hours, removing the lid for the last 20 minutes of the cooking time to crisp the top. Serve immediately.

MEATLOAF

Serves 12

INGREDIENTS
400g/14oz minced pork
225g/8oz lean minced beef
50ml/2fl oz single cream
75g/3oz ground pork rinds
1 eggs
1/4 tsp hot chilli oil
Salt and pepper
1/2 tsp ground sage
3 tsp dried minced onion
2 tbsp dried parsley flakes
1/2 tsp mustard powder
1/8 tsp sugar substitute

Preheat the oven to 180°C/350°F/Gas mark 4.

In a large mixing bowl thoroughly combine all the ingredients
with an electric mixer on low speed. Place the mixture into a loaf
pan and bake in the oven for 1 hour.

Remove the meatloaf from the oven and remove any excess
grease from the top with a spoon. Bake for a further 15 to 20
minutes and serve hot.

ROAST CHICKEN WITH STUFFING

Serves 5

INGREDIENTS
Vegetable oil, for greasing
15g/1/2oz butter
3 rashers back bacon, chopped
1 onion, finely chopped
1 courgette, grated and squeezed of excess fluid
75g/3oz fresh parsley, finely chopped
1 tbsp lemon juice
1 tbsp chopped fresh rosemary
Salt and pepper
1 medium whole chicken
50ml/2fl oz vegetable oil
Grated zest of 1/2 lemon

Preheat the oven to 180°C/350°F/Gas mark 4. Lightly grease a
large baking tray with oil.

Heat the butter in a frying pan, add the bacon and onion and
stir-fry for 3 minutes. Add the courgette and stir-fry for a further
5 minutes or until all fluid has evaporated. In a large mixing
bowl, combine the contents of the frying pan with the parsley,
lemon juice, rosemary and seasoning.

Stuff the chicken with the stuffing mixture and close with
skewers. Cover chicken in vegetable oil, rub in the lemon zest
and seasoning. Place chicken on the prepared baking tray and
cook in the oven for 1 hour or until the juices run clear.

BEEF-STUFFED CABBAGE

Serves 6

INGREDIENTS
1 head white cabbage
1.3kg/3lb lean minced beef
1 small onion, grated
450g/1lb passata
Salt and pepper
75ml/3fl oz whipping cream
1 tbsp clear honey
50ml/2fl oz white wine vinegar
75g/3oz fresh parsley, chopped

Remove the core from the cabbage head, keeping the head whole. Bring a large pot of salted water to the boil and cook the cabbage in for 5 minutes. Remove from the pan and pull off 12 whole leaves from the cabbage head.

In a medium-sized bowl, combine the beef, onion, half the passata and seasoning and blend well.

Place the cabbage leaves in a large bowl. Bring a large pot of water to the boil, then immediately cover the cabbage with the boiled water. Let stand for 5 minutes, then drain well.

Shape the meat mixture into 12 miniature loaf shapes. Place a loaf in the centre of each cabbage leaf, then roll up. Place the rolls, seam side down, in a large frying pan.

In a bowl, combine the cream, honey, vinegar, parsley and the remaining tomato sauce. Pour this mixture evenly over the cabbage rolls. Bring to the boil, the reduce the heat, cover and simmer for 1 to 1½ hours. Serve hot.

CURRIED CHICKEN

Serves 4

INGREDIENTS
4 chicken quarters, skinned and chopped
1 onion, finely chopped
15g/1/2oz butter
1 tbsp curry powder
225ml/8fl oz double cream
4 garlic cloves, crushed
125ml/4fl oz water

Preheat the oven to 190°C/375°F/Gas mark 5.

Arrange the chicken quarters in a shallow baking dish and scatter the onion over the top.

Melt the butter in a frying pan and sauté the curry powder in it for 2 minutes.

In a bowl mix together the cream, garlic, water and curry powder, and pour this mixture over the chicken. Bake in the oven for 1 to 1½ hours, turning the chicken halfway through, so that the sauce flavours both sides.

Remove all the chicken from the pan and place on a serving platter. Take the sauce in the baking dish and scrape it all into a blender or food processor. Blend it with a little more water to get a nice, rich, golden sauce. Pour it over the chicken and serve immediately.

CHINESE BEEF WITH BROCCOLI

Serves 8

INGREDIENTS
1 tbsp coconut oil
1¹/₂lb top sirloin steak, cut into strips
³/₄ tsp seasoning salt
1 tsp minced garlic
¹/₄ tsp lemon pepper
¹/₄ tsp ground ginger
900g/2lb bag frozen chopped broccoli
3 tbsp soy sauce
1¹/₂ tsp sesame oil
¹/₈ tsp chilli oil

Heat the coconut oil in a wok over a high heat. Add the beef and seasonings, stirring well to coat the meat evenly. Continue cooking the meat until it is no longer red.

Add the frozen broccoli to the pan and stir well. Cover and leave to steam for 4 minutes, stirring occasionally, until the broccoli is heated through.

Add the soy sauce, sesame oil and chilli oil to the pan. Heat through, stirring well. Serve hot.

CHINESE PORK

Serves 3

INGREDIENTS
2 tbsp soy sauce
2 tbsp Thai fish sauce
1 tsp sugar substitute
1/4 tsp guar gum
2 tsp dried basil
1 1/2 tsp chilli flakes
2 tbsp rapeseed oil
2 garlic cloves, crushed
1 onion, sliced
3 boneless, skinless chicken breasts, cut into 1cm/1/2in cubes
250g/9oz frozen, sliced green beans

Combine the soy sauce, fish sauce, sugar substitute and guar gum
in a blender or food processor. Blend for several seconds, then
turn off the blender, add the basil and chilli flakes and set aside.

Heat the oil in a wok over a high heat. When the oil is hot, add the
garlic, onion and chicken, and stir-fry for 4 minutes. Add the
beans and continue to stir-fry until the chicken is cooked through.

Stir the seasoning mixture from the blender into the wok, turn
the heat to medium, cover and leave to simmer for 3 minutes,
then serve.

RUSSIAN-STYLE BEEF

Serves 3

INGREDIENTS
450g/1lb minced beef
1 garlic clove, crushed
1 onion, diced
100g/4oz mushrooms, chopped
1 tsp beef stock powder
2 tbsp Worcestershire sauce
1 tsp paprika
200ml/7fl oz sour cream
Salt and pepper

In a heavy frying pan over a medium heat, brown and crumble the beef. Add the garlic and onion and cook until all pinkness is gone from the beef.

Drain excess grease from the pan and add the mushrooms, stock powder, Worcestershire sauce and paprika, cook, stirring, until the mushrooms are cooked. Just before serving, stir in the sour cream, then season to taste. Heat through without boiling, then serve hot.

ROAST DUCK

Serves 6

INGREDIENTS
3 lemons
Salt and pepper
2kg/4 1/2lb ready-to-cook duck
3 tbsp butter
2 tsp sugar
2 tbsp white wine vinegar
450ml/3/4pt chicken stock
3 tbsp dry sherry

Preheat the oven to 190°C/375°F/Gas mark 5.

Cut the zest from 2 of the lemons as thinly as possible. Juice 1 of the lemons and reserve the juice. Separate the other lemon into segments and set aside. Cut the zest into narrow strips and cook in boiling water for 5 minutes. Rinse with cold water and pat dry.

Season the inside and outside of the duck with salt and pepper. Place half of the lemon rind and half the butter in the cavity, then tie the legs together with a piece of butcher's twine. Place the duck on a rack in a large roasting pan.

Roast the duck, uncovered, for 1¼ hours. Baste the duck with its natural juices during roasting. Let the duck rest for at least 30 minutes before serving.

In a saucepan over a medium heat, cook the sugar and vinegar together until a caramel has formed, stirring often. Add the stock, the reserved lemon juice and the remaining lemon zest strips. Add the sherry and any juices in the roasting pan from the duck and simmer over a medium heat until the sauce has thickened. Add the lemon segments and the remaining butter and simmer for a further 5 minutes.

Serve the duck sliced and drizzled with the sauce and garnished with lemon.

SPICY PORK

Serves 2

INGREDIENTS
350g/12oz pork tenderloin, visible fat removed
50ml/2fl oz soy sauce
50ml/2fl oz white wine vinegar
4 tsp Dijon mustard
4 garlic cloves, crushed
2 tsp ground ginger

Line a baking tray with aluminium foil. Cut the pork almost in half lengthwise and open like a book. Be careful not to cut all the way through.

Combine the soy sauce, vinegar, mustard, garlic and ginger in a small bowl. Add the pork and leave to marinate for 20 minutes. Remove from the marinade and place the pork on the prepared baking tray. Place under a hot grill and cook for 5 minutes, then turn and grill for a further 3 minutes. Check the pork is cooked, then slice and serve.

LEMON PEPPER CHICKEN

Serves 4

INGREDIENTS
1¹/₂ tbsp lard
800g/1lb 12oz boneless, skinless chicken breasts
Salt and lemon pepper

Melt the lard in a large frying pan over a medium heat. Season the chicken on one side with the salt and lemon pepper. Place the chicken into the pan seasoned-side down, then liberally season the other side.

Cook the chicken in the frying pan until it begins to brown on one side, then turn it over and brown the other side. Continue cooking and turning for about 35 minutes, or until done. Serve hot.

CHICKEN WITH PEANUT

Serves 3

INGREDIENTS
1 tsp ground cumin
1/2 tsp ground cinnamon
3 boneless, skinless chicken breasts
3 tbsp peanut oil
1/2 onion, thinly sliced
400g/14oz canned chopped tomatoes
1 tbsp lemon juice
2 tbsp smooth peanut butter
2 garlic cloves, crushed
1 red chilli, halved and seeded

On a saucer or plate, stir the cumin and cinnamon together, then rub into both sides of chicken breasts.

Place the oil in a large frying pan over a medium heat and add the chicken and onion. Brown the chicken a little on both sides.

Place all the tomato liquid and half the tomatoes in a blender or food processor with the lemon juice, peanut butter, garlic and chilli. Blend or process until smooth.

Pour this sauce over the chicken, and add the remaining tomatoes. Cover, then turn the heat down to low and leave to gently simmer for 10 to 15 minutes, or until the chicken is cooked through.

LAMB STIR-FRY

Serves 4

INGREDIENTS
3 red peppers. quartered
2 tbsp olive oil
3 baby aubergines, peeled and sliced
1 fennel bulb, sliced
400g/14oz lamb neck fillet, thinly sliced
2 garlic cloves, crushed
1/4 tsp Tabasco sauce
1 tbsp fresh oregano, chopped
Salt and pepper
1 tbsp white wine vinegar
6 slices prosciutto, roughly chopped
75g/3oz fresh parsley, chopped

Place the red peppers under a grill, skin-side up. Grill until the skin blackens and blisters. Remove from the grill and allow to cool before peeling.

Heat the oil in a large wok, add the aubergine and fennel, and stir-fry for 5 minutes or until cooked through. Remove from wok and reserve.

Add the lamb in batches to the wok with the garlic, Tabasco sauce, oregano and seasoning. Stir-fry lamb until browned and cooked through.

Chop the red peppers and add to the wok with the fennel, aubergine, vinegar, prosciutto and parsley and stir-fry a further 3 minutes. Serve immediately.

FAJITAS

Serves 4

INGREDIENTS
125ml/4fl oz lite or alchol-free beer
125ml/4fl oz olive oil
2 tbsp lime juice
1/2 onion, thinly sliced
1 tsp chilli flakes
1/4 tsp ground cumin
1/4 tsp freshly ground black pepper
650g/1lb 9oz rib-eye steak
1 tbsp vegetable oil
1 green pepper, sliced
1 onion, thickly sliced

To make the marinade mix together the beer, olive oil, lime juice, onion, chilli flakes, cumin and pepper.

Place the steak in a large plastic bag and pour the marinade over it. Seal the bag, pressing out the air and place it in the refrigerator. Leave to marinate for at least 3 hours.

When ready to cook, remove your steak from the bag, reserving a couple of tablespoons of the marinade. Slice your steak quite thinly, across the grain.

Heat the vegetable oil to a large frying pan over a high heat. Add the steak slices, pepper and onion. Stir-fry them until the meat is cooked through.

Stir in the reserved marinade and serve with low-carb tortillas, guacamole, salsa and sour cream.

BEEF PROVENÇAL

Serves 4

INGREDIENTS
100g/4oz back bacon, chopped
2 onions, quartered
900g/2lb rump steak, cut into 5cm/2in cubes
1 fennel bulb, trimmed and thinly sliced
4 garlic cloves
6 strips of orange zest
1 bay leaf
1/4 tsp dried basil
1/4 tsp dried thyme
1/4 tsp dried parsley
250ml/9fl oz red wine
225ml/8fl oz beef stock

Using a large frying pan, cook the bacon over a medium heat until crispy. Remove with a slotted spoon and reserve. Remove half of the bacon fat and reserve.

Raise the heat to medium-high and cook the onions until lightly browned. Add the steak and brown on all sides, adding additional bacon fat as needed. Remove the steak and onions and any juices and reserve.

Add the fennel, garlic, orange zest, bay leaf and dried herbs with a little more bacon fat. Cook until the vegetables are tender. Add the steak, onions, red wine and stock. Bring to a simmer and cook, covered, over a low heat. Braise for about 2 hours or until the meat begins to fall apart, skimming off any fat that rises to the surface.

Serve in warm bowls garnished with the bacon.

SPICY MINCE

Serves 6

INGREDIENTS
900g/2lb minced beef
3 garlic cloves, crushed
100g/4oz onion, chopped
400g/14oz canned chopped tomatoes
125ml/4fl oz tomato sauce
4 tsp ground cumin
2 tsp dried oregano
2 tsp unsweetened cocoa powder
1 tsp paprika

In a heavy frying pan over a medium-high heat, brown and crumble the beef. Pour off any excess grease and add the garlic, onion, tomatoes, tomato sauce, cumin, oregano, cocoa and paprika. Stir well to combine.

Turn the heat down to low, then cover and simmer for 30 minutes. Uncover and simmer for a further 20 minutes, or until the chilli thickens. Serve immediately.

LAMB STEW

Serves 4

INGREDIENTS
3 tbsp olive oil
650g/1lb 7oz lean stewing lamb, cut into chunks
250g/9oz turnip, diced
100g/4oz onion, chopped
250g/9oz swede, diced
200ml/7fl oz beef stock
$1/2$ tsp guar gum
Salt and pepper
1 bay leaf
3 garlic cloves, crushed

Put the oil in a heavy frying pan over a medium-high heat and brown the lamb in the oil. Add the turnip, onion and swede.

Put the beef stock and guar gum in a blender or food processor and blend for 30 seconds. Pour the mixture into the frying pan and add the seasoning, bay leaf and garlic and stir.

Cover, turn the heat down to low and leave to simmer for 1 hour. Serve hot.

CURRIED VEAL

Serves 4

INGREDIENTS
625g/1lb 6oz veal topside
2 tsp curry powder
1 tsp cumin
1 tsp coriander powder
1 tsp paprika
2 tbsp olive oil
8 yellow squash, quartered
2 yellow courgettes, quartered
1 stick lemongrass, finely chopped
1 tsp fresh ginger, crushed
$3/4$ tsp ground turmeric powder
1 tsp curry powder
1 red chilli, seeded and finely chopped
Salt and pepper
175ml/6fl oz vegetable stock
2 tomatoes, diced
175ml/6fl oz sour cream
50g/2oz fresh coriander leaves, chopped

Preheat the oven to 180°C/350°F/Gas mark 4.

Roll veal in curry powder, cumin, coriander powder and paprika.
Heat the oil in a large saucepan, add the meat and sear on all
sides. Place meat on baking tray and cook in the oven for 30
minutes. Set aside for 10 minutes before slicing.

To the saucepan, add the squash and courgette, then stir-fry for 5
minutes over a high heat until lightly browned. To the vegetables,
add the lemongrass, ginger, turmeric, curry powder, chilli and
seasoning, then stir-fry for 1 minute. Add the stock and tomatoes
and simmer uncovered for 20 minutes.

Stir through the sour cream and coriander and heat through.
Serve the sliced veal with the curried vegetables.

BACON AND CHEESE OMELETTE

Serves 6

INGREDIENTS
2 tbsp olive oil
4 rashers back bacon, chopped, rind removed
20 mushrooms, sliced
9 eggs
225g/8oz Cheddar cheese, grated
100g/4oz Parmesan cheese, grated
175ml/6fl oz double cream
3/4 tsp ground nutmeg
75g/3oz fresh parsley, finely chopped
Salt and pepper

Preheat the oven to 180°C/350°F/Gas mark 4.

Heat the olive oil in a saucepan, add the bacon and mushrooms and fry for 5 minutes, or until the bacon is well browned. Remove the bacon and mushrooms from the pan and place in a casserole dish. Add the eggs, cheeses, cream, nutmeg and mix well, seasoning to taste.

Cook in the oven for 45 minutes or until the egg is set and the omelette is well browned.

CHICKEN WITH FETA CHEESE

Serves 4

INGREDIENTS
2 tbsp olive oil
3 chicken breasts, thinly sliced
2 garlic cloves, crushed
1 red onion, sliced
2 small fennel bulbs, sliced
2 tsp fresh thyme
200ml/7fl oz chicken stock
125ml/4fl oz single cream
100g/4oz feta cheese, crumbled
Salt and pepper

Heat the oil in a large wok and stir-fry the chicken until browned all over. Remove the chicken from the wok and reserve.

Add the garlic and onion to the wok and stir-fry 3 minutes until onion softens. Add the fennel and thyme and stir-fry for a further 5 minutes.

Return the chicken to the wok and add the stock and seasoning, then bring to the boil. Reduce the heat and simmer for 10 minutes, or until fluid has condensed.

Add the cream and cheese and heat through gently before serving.

BARBECUE CHICKEN

Serves 4

INGREDIENTS
1 small onion, chopped
3 tbsp tomato purée
2 tsp grated fresh ginger
2 garlic cloves, crushed
1/4 tsp cayenne pepper
1 tsp ground coriander
1 tsp cumin seeds
1 tsp garam masala
Salt and pepper
4 breast chicken fillets, skinned
1 lemon, cut into wedges

Preheat the oven to 200°C/400°F/Gas mark 6.

Combine the ginger, garlic, cayenne pepper, coriander, cumin seeds, garam masala and seasoning to taste in a blender or food processor until they form a paste.

Baste the chicken fillets in the paste, then place in a sealed container and leave in the refrigerator overnight.

Bake the chicken in the oven for 30 minutes. Turn over and coat with more marinade, then bake for a further 15 minutes and serve with the lemon wedges.

Spicy pork (see page 53)

Above, Yogurt parfait (see page 110); Right, Spicy chicken salad (see page 37)

Above, Chicken wings (see page 121); Below, Guacamole (see page 125)

Above, Roast chicken (see page 47); Right, Peach frozen yogurt (see page 111)

Above, Tomato soup (see page 21); Below, Scampi (see page 88)

Above, Tofu and vegetables (see page 99); Right, Fruit salad (see page 116)

Above, Chinese beef with broccoli (see page 50); Below, Stir-fry chicken (see page 44)

Baked bananas (see page 115)

CHILLI CON CARNE

Serves 4

INGREDIENTS
100g/4oz red kidney beans
1 garlic clove, crushed
1 onion, coarsely chopped
1 tbsp olive oil
450g/1lb minced beef
50g/2oz green pepper, chopped
225g/8oz tomatoes, chopped
1 tsp chilli powder
1 tsp chopped oregano
2 bay leaves
1 tsp chopped parsley
Salt and pepper

Place the kidney beans in a bowl and add enough water to cover. Leave to soak overnight, then drain well.

Place the beans in a pan with 1.2 litres/2pts fresh water and boil vigorously for 30 minutes. Drain and discard the water, and replace with 600ml/1pt fresh water, then boil for a further 1 hour, until the beans are tender.

Fry the garlic and onion in the olive oil until soft. Add the minced beef and fry until brown.

Add the green pepper, tomatoes, chilli powder, oregano, bay leaves, parsley, seasoning and 300ml/1/2pt water, then simmer gently for 30 to 45 minds. Drain the cooked kidney beans, add them to the pan and simmer for a further 30 minutes before serving.

TURKEY LOAF

Serves 6

INGREDIENTS
For the loaf:
3 courgettes, trimmed and cut into thin ribbons
1 onion, finely chopped
2 garlic cloves, crushed
900g/2lb minced turkey
2 tbsp chopped fresh parsley
1 tbsp chopped fresh rosemary
2 tbsp chopped fresh chives
1 egg white, lightly beaten
Salt and pepper

Preheat the oven to 190°C/375°F/Gas mark 5. Line a 30cm/12in loaf tin with greaseproof paper.

Add the courgettes to a saucepan of boiling water and blanch over a high heat for 1 minute, then drain and rinse.

Line the prepared tin with the courgettes, ensuring that there are no gaps.

Put the onion, garlic and turkey in a bowl with the parsley, rosemary, chives and egg white and combine thoroughly. Season with salt and pepper.

Place the turkey mixture into the base of the tin and level it off.

Now cover the courgettes with the remaining turkey mixture. Press it all firmly down and then cover with a very thick layer of baking paper.

Set the terrine tin in a deep baking tin with enough water to come one third of the way up the loaf tin. Place in the oven and bake for 1 1/2 hours, until the loaf is cooked through and the juices are clear.

CHICKEN AND SWEET POTATO BAKE

Serves 4

INGREDIENTS
4 chicken breasts
1 tsp ground ginger
1/2 tsp ground nutmeg
1/2 tsp black pepper
3 sweet potatoes, cut into small pieces
2 tsp orange zest
250ml/9fl oz apple juice

Preheat oven to 200°C/400°F/Gas mark 6.

In a small bowl mix together the ginger, nutmeg and pepper, then sprinkle on both sides of the chicken breasts and place in baking dish.

Place the sweet potatoes around chicken and sprinkle any of the remaining spice mixture over the chicken and potatoes. Sprinkle orange zest over everything, then pour apple juice over.

Bake in the oven for 45 minutes, or until the chicken is cooked. Serve hot.

FISH MAIN COURSES

For something a bit different, why not try a fish main course instead of a meat-based one. There is still plenty of variety to be found within the recipes in this section, from classics such as bouillabaisse to Thai fish and crab stir-fry. If you cannot face filleting fish yourself, you can either buy it prepared and chilled from the supermarket or, if you prefer fresh, get your fishmonger to fillet it for you. There are also a range of cooking techniques here, such as steaming and baking, so you can learn new skills in the kitchen.

SALMON PARCELS

Serves 6

INGREDIENTS
25ml/1fl oz groundnut oil
2 yellow peppers, thinly sliced
1 large fennel bulb, thinly sliced
5cm/2in piece fresh ginger, peeled and grated
1 green chilli, seeded and shredded
2 leeks, shredded lengthways
2 tbsp chopped fresh chives
2 tsp soy sauce
Salt and pepper
6 salmon fillets, about 150g/5oz each, skinned
2 tsp sesame oil

Preheat the oven to 190°C/375°F/Gas mark 5. Cut six 35cm/14in
rounds of greaseproof paper and set aside.

Heat the groundnut oil in a large frying pan. Add the peppers,
fennel and ginger and cook, stirring occasionally, for 5 minutes.

Add the chilli and leeks to the pan and cook, stirring occasionally,
for about 3 minutes. Stir in half the chives and the soy sauce and
season to taste. Set the vegetable mixture aside to cool slightly.

When the vegetable mixture is cool, divide it equally among the
greaseproof paper rounds and top with a portion of salmon.
Drizzle each portion with sesame oil and sprinkle with the
remaining chives.

Fold the baking parchment over the fish, twisting the edges
together to seal.

Place the parcels on a baking tray and bake for 15 to 20 minutes.
Carefully transfer the parcels to serving plates and serve
immediately.

PRAWN JAMBALAYA

Serves 6

INGREDIENTS
350g/12oz smoked sausage, sliced 1cm/¹/₂in thick
75ml/3fl oz olive oil
2 garlic cloves, crushed
150g/5oz onion, chopped
1 green pepper, diced
400g/14oz canned chopped tomatoes
225ml/8fl oz chicken stock
1 tsp dried thyme
1 cauliflower, broken into florets
225g/8oz shelled, deveined prawns
Salt and pepper

In a large frying pan, start browning the sausage in the olive oil.
When it is lightly golden, add the garlic, onion and green pepper.
Sauté the vegetables until the onion becomes translucent.

Add the tomatoes, chicken stock and thyme and simmer,
uncovered, for 20 minutes.

Add the cauliflower and simmer for a further 15 minutes.

Add the prawns and simmer for a further 5 minutes. Season to
taste and serve.

GINGER SCALLOPS

Serves 4

INGREDIENTS
1 tsp butter
4 tsp olive oil
1/2 leek, trimmed and chopped
3 shallots, very finely chopped
50ml/2fl oz sake
125ml/4fl oz vegetable stock
3 tbsp peeled and sliced fresh ginger
25g/1oz fresh parsley, chopped
225ml/8fl oz sour cream
1 tsp grated fresh ginger
Salt and pepper
8 sea scallops, trimmed and halved

Melt the butter and 1 teaspoon oil in a frying pan over a medium heat. Add the leeks and cook for 3 minutes, stirring frequently. Remove from the pan and keep warm.

Heat 2 teaspoons oil over a medium heat. Add the shallots and cook for 2 minutes or until lightly browned. Add the sake, stock, sliced ginger and parsley. Cook until the liquid reduces by half.

Strain the sauce through a sieve into a saucepan. Place over a medium heat and whisk in the sour cream. Cook for 3 minutes, whisking constantly. Add the grated ginger and season to taste. Remove from the heat and keep warm.

Lightly brush a large frying pan with the remaining oil and place over a high heat. Season the scallops and cook in the hot pan, uncovered, for 2 minutes.

Place the leeks in the centre of four serving plates. Place the scallops around the leeks and spoon the sauce over the top. Serve immediately.

CRAB STIR-FRY

Serves 2

INGREDIENTS
375g/13oz crabmeat, drained
50g/2oz tomato purée
1/2 tsp hot pepper sauce
125ml/4fl oz water
1/2 tsp sugar substitute
4 tsp rapeseed oil
2 garlic cloves, crushed
50g/2oz shallots, chopped
2 tbsp chopped fresh ginger
4 lemongrass stalks, sliced
225g/8oz fresh beansprouts
225g/8oz mangetout, trimmed
2 tbsp unsalted roasted peanuts, chopped

Flake the crabmeat with a fork into a bowl. Combine the tomato purée, hot pepper sauce, water and sugar substitute in a small bowl and set aside.

Heat the oil in a large frying pan over a high heat. Add the garlic, shallots, ginger and lemongrass and stir-fry for 2 minutes. Add the beansprouts, mangetout and crabmeat and stir-fry for a further 3 minutes.

Add the sauce and toss through for an additional 1 minute. Remove to serving plates, sprinkle with the peanuts, and serve.

THAI FISH

Serves 4

INGREDIENTS
200g/7oz beansprouts
1 tsp green curry paste
1 tbsp Thai fish sauce
225ml/8fl oz coconut milk
4 snapper fillets, about 200g/7oz each
1 tbsp rapeseed oil
2 lemongrass stalks, finely chopped
250g/9oz mangetout, trimmed
25g/1oz basil, finely chopped
100g/4oz baby spinach

Soak beansprouts in fresh water for at least 10 minutes.
In a large bowl, mix the curry paste, fish sauce and coconut milk.
Add the snapper and marinate for at least 30 minutes.

Heat a frying pan over a medium heat and add 2 teaspoons
rapeseed oil. When the oil is hot, add the fillets, reserving the
marinade. Cook for 2 minutes each side, then remove from the
pan and keep warm.

Wipe the pan clean and add the remaining oil and increase the
heat. Add the lemongrass and stir-fry for 1 minute. Reduce the
heat and add marinade, mangetout, beansprouts and basil.
Return the snapper to the pan. Cover and gently simmer for 2
minutes. Remove from heat and serve topped with the spinach.

JAPANESE TUNA STEAKS

Serves 4

INGREDIENTS
1 tbsp grated fresh ginger root
1 tsp wasabi
3 tbsp lemon juice
3 tbsp soy sauce
2 tbsp finely chopped coriander
4 tuna steaks, about 200g/7oz each
Sesame oil, for brushing
2 courgettes, sliced
2 carrots, sliced
1 red pepper, sliced

In a screw-top jar, combine the ginger, wasabi, lemon juice, soy sauce and coriander. Shake well, then pour into a large bowl and add the tuna. Leave to marinate for at least 30 minutes.

Heat a large frying pan over a medium-high heat and brush with a little sesame oil. Add the tuna, reserving the marinade, and cook for 3 minutes each side until medium-rare, or longer according to taste.

Heat a separate frying pan over a medium heat. When hot brush with a little oil. Add the vegetables and stir-fry over a high heat for 3 minutes, shaking constantly. Remove from the heat and add half the reserved marinade. Shake vigorously to combine the marinade and vegetables.

To serve, arrange vegetables in the centre of each serving plate and position the tuna on top. Drizzle the remaining marinade over the top and serve.

PRAWNS IN BLANKETS

Serves 4

INGREDIENTS
675g/1½lb raw king prawns
10 slices pancetta, halved
28 fresh sage leaves
75ml/3fl oz sherry vinegar

Remove the shells and tails from the prawns and devein them.

On a flat surface, lay out half a slice of pancetta. Place a sage leaf on top, then place a prawn across the pancetta and sage. Roll the pancetta around the prawn and secure it with a toothpick. Repeat with the remaining prawns.

Heat a medium frying pan over a medium-high heat. Place half of the rolled prawns in the pan. Cook until the pancetta is light brown and crispy on each side. Place the prawns on kitchen paper to drain, and keep warm. Repeat for the remaining rolled prawns.

When all the prawns are cooked, keep the pan over the heat and pour in the vinegar and cook down until syrupy. Place the prawns on a platter and pour the hot vinegar over the top. Serve immediately.

BOUILLABAISSE

Serves 2

INGREDIENTS
3 tbsp olive oil
75g/3oz onion, chopped
75g/3oz leeks, finely chopped
1 celery stalk, finely chopped
1 garlic clove, crushed
1 bouquet garni
1/2 tsp orange zest
1/4 tsp fennel seeds
100g/4oz tomatoes, skinned and roughly chopped
Pinch of saffron threads, soaked in 2 tbsp hot water
500ml/16fl oz fish stock
350g/12oz red mullet fillets, cut into chunks
400g/14oz monkfish fillets, cut into chunks
2 tsp tomato purée
1 tsp Pernod
Salt and pepper
2 tbsp chopped parsley, to garnish

Heat the oil in a large saucepan, add the onion, leeks and celery and cook for 5 minutes until softened.

Add the garlic, bouquet garni, orange zest, fennel seeds and tomatoes. Stir in the saffron and its liquid and the fish stock. Bring to the boil, then reduce the heat and simmer, covered, for 35 minutes.

Add the fish and cook for 5 to 10 minutes, or until all the fish flakes easily. Transfer the fish to a plate with a slotted spoon.

Keep the liquid boiling and add the tomato purée and Pernod.

Adjust the seasoning, then serve the soup topped with the fish and garnished with parsley.

GINGER SALMON

Serves 2

INGREDIENTS
2 tbsp olive oil
350g/12oz salmon fillet
Salt and pepper
2 tbsp low-sodium soy sauce
2 tbsp water
2 tbsp chopped fresh ginger

Heat the oil in a frying pan over a medium-high heat. Add the salmon and brown for 2 minutes. Turn, season the cooked side, then brown the second side. Lower the heat and sauté for 5 minutes.

Combine the soy sauce, water and ginger in a small bowl.

Remove the salmon from the pan, add the soy sauce mixture to the pan and cook for several seconds. Spoon the sauce over the salmon to serve.

PRAWN CURRY

Serves 4

INGREDIENTS
125ml/4fl oz fish stock
4 fresh lemon myrtle leaves
4 tbsp rapeseed oil
1 tsp sesame oil
1 garlic clove, crushed
1 onion, finely chopped
2 tsp fresh ginger, finely chopped
1 tbsp red curry paste
32 large raw king prawns, peeled and deveined
4 tbsp Thai fish sauce
Salt and pepper
3 tbsp sour cream
25g/1oz fresh basil leaves, chopped
1 bunch fresh coriander leaves, chopped
4 spring onions, sliced

Heat the stock in a saucepan, then add the lemon myrtle leaves
and leave to stand for 20 minutes.

Heat the oils in a large wok. Add the garlic, onion and ginger and
stir-fry for 2 minutes. Add the red curry paste and stir-fry for 1
minute, then add the prawns and stir-fry for a further 1 minute.

Add the fish sauce, seasoning, stock and lemon myrtle leaves to
the wok and bring to the boil. Reduce the heat and add the sour
cream, basil, coriander and spring onions. Heat through gently
and serve.

SCAMPI

Serves 3

INGREDIENTS
100g/3oz butter
75ml/3fl oz olive oil
3 garlic cloves, crushed
450g/1lb raw prawns
75ml/3fl oz dry white wine
1 1/2 tbsp finely chopped fresh parsley

Melt the butter with the olive oil in a heavy frying pan over a medium-low heat. Add the garlic and stir.

Add the prawns to the pan and cook for 5 to 6 minutes.

Add the wine and simmer for a further 2 minutes, then serve garnished with the parsley.

STEAMED TROUT

Serves 6

INGREDIENTS

2 trout, about 700g/1lb 9oz each
1½ tsp salted black beans
½ tsp granulated sugar
2 tbsp finely shredded fresh ginger
4 garlic cloves, thinly sliced
2 tbsp sake, or dry sherry
2 tbsp soy sauce
5 spring onions, finely sliced
3 tbsp groundnut oil
2 tsp sesame oil

Wash the fish inside and out under cold running water, then pat dry with kitchen paper. Using a sharp knife, slash 4 deep crosses on each side of each fish.

Place half the black beans and the sugar in a small bowl and mash together. Stir in the remaining whole beans.

Place a little ginger and garlic inside the cavity of each fish, then lay them on a plate or dish that will fit inside a large steamer. Rub the bean mixture into the fish, then sprinkle the remaining ginger and garlic over the top. Cover with clingfilm and place the fish in the refrigerator for at least 1 hour.

Place the steamer over a pan of boiling water. Sprinkle the sake or sherry and half the soy sauce over the fish and place the plate of fish inside the steamer. Steam for 20 minutes, or until the fish is just cooked and the flesh flakes easily. Carefully lift the fish on to a serving dish. Sprinkle the fish with the remaining soy sauce and the spring onions.

In a small pan, heat the groundnut oil until very hot, then pour it over the fish. Lightly sprinkle the sesame oil over the top and serve immediately.

BAKED HADDOCK

Serves 2

INGREDIENTS

1 egg
1 tbsp milk
2 haddock fillets, about 200g/7oz each
2 tbsp grated Parmesan cheese
1 tbsp breadcrumbs
1 tbsp olive oil
25g/1oz butter, divided
1 tsp grated lemon zest
2 tbsp chopped fresh parsley

In a large glass bowl, beat the egg with the milk. Place the haddock in the mixture and leave in the refrigerator to soak for 1 hour.

Preheat the oven to 190°C/375°F/Gas mark 5.

In a separate bowl mix together the Parmesan and breadcrumbs. Remove the haddock from the egg wash, shaking off any excess, and dip it into the breadcrumb mixture, lightly coating each fillet.

In a frying pan, heat the oil and 1 tablespoon butter over a medium heat until it just starts to foam. Add the haddock and lightly brown on both sides. Place the frying pan in the oven and bake for 10 minutes or until cooked through.

Remove the haddock from the sauté pan and keep it warm while preparing the sauce. Melt the remaining butter in the same frying pan, scraping the bottom of the pan. Add the lemon zest and parsley. Cook over a medium heat, stirring constantly for 2 minutes.

Pour the butter sauce over each fillet and serve immediately.

CRAB SPAGHETTI

Serves 4

INGREDIENTS

350g/12oz wholewheat spaghetti
1 tsp olive oil
2 garlic cloves, crushed
75g/3oz spring onions, sliced
1 red chilli, seeded and finely sliced
300g/11oz cooked white crabmeat
Grated zest and juice of 1 lemon
6 tbsp crème fraîche
Salt and pepper

Cook the spaghetti in a large saucepan of salted boiling water according to the package instructions. Drain well and rinse.

Heat the oil in a large frying pan, then add the garlic, spring onions and chilli and fry for 3 minutes. Add the crabmeat, lemon zest and juice crème fraîche and pasta. Season to taste and heat through to serve.

ROAST TROUT

Serves 4

INGREDIENTS

4 ocean trout fillets
2 tsp sesame oil
Salt and pepper
3/4 cup sour cream
1 tsp fresh ginger, minced
1 tsp wasabi paste
1/2 lime juice
300g/11oz English spinach leaves, trimmed and washed

Preheat the oven to 140°C/275°F/Gas mark 1.

Place the trout on a baking tray. Brush with sesame oil and sprinkle with a little salt. Bake in the oven for 30 minutes. Combine the sour cream, ginger, wasabi and lime juice, then set aside.

Steam the spinach briefly, drain and divide between four serving plates. Serve the trout on top of the spinach, garnish with wasabi dressing.

FISH PIE

Serves 4

INGREDIENTS

900g/2lb smoked cod fillets, skinned and bones removed
600ml/1pt skimmed milk
1 bay leaf
100g/4oz button mushrooms, quartered
100g/4oz frozen corn kernels
100g/4oz frozen peas
550g/1lb 4oz leeks, sliced
5 tbsp half-fat crème fraîche

3 tbsp cornflour
25g/1oz Cheddar cheese, grated
Salt and pepper

Preheat the oven to 200°C/400°F/Gas mark 6.

Place the cod in a large frying pan with the milk and bay leaf
and slowly bring to the boil. Reduce the heat and simmer for 5
minutes. Remove the pan from the heat, then transfer the fish to
a baking dish and flake into pieces.

Add the mushrooms, corn kernels and peas to the milk remaining in the frying pan and bring back to the boil. Reduce the heat
and simmer gently for 5 minutes.

Remove the vegetables with a slotted spoon and transfer them to
the baking dish. Strain off 300ml/1/2pt of the milk and reserve.

Put the leeks in a clean frying pan with 75ml/3fl oz water. Bring
to the boil, reduce the heat and simmer for 8 minutes, stirring
occasionally, until softened. Remove from the heat and let cool
before stirring in the crème fraîche.

Blend the cornflour to a smooth paste with a little of the reserved
milk. Put the remainder of the reserved milk. Put the remainder
of the milk in the saucepan and bring to the boil. Stir the paste
into the boiling milk and stir until thickened. Pour the sauce over
the fish mixture and mix lightly.

Spoon the leeks over the top of the fish. Sprinkle with the
cheese, then bake in the oven for 30 minutes, until bubbling.

VEGGIE MAIN COURSES

If you are following a vegetarian diet and a low-carb diet then you might find it twice as hard to find recipes that fit both criteria, let alone ones that are interesting and tasty as well. Here are several vegetarian main courses that are low in carbohydrates, including ratatouille, courgette casserole and stuffed aubergines. Some dishes are made up from vegetables, while others feature ingredients such as nuts, cheese and tofu as the main ingredients. Even if you are not a vegetarian, why not try some of these recipes as a healthy variation?

VEGETABLE CASSEROLE

Serves 6

INGREDIENTS
50ml/2fl oz extra-virgin olive oil
1 onion, chopped
400g/14oz canned chopped tomatoes
2 garlic cloves, finely chopped
25g/1oz fresh basil, chopped
Salt and pepper
1 aubergine, peeled and sliced
3 courgettes, sliced
2 red peppers, quartered
225g/8oz Mozzarella cheese, thinly sliced
75g/3oz dried breadcrumbs
100g/4oz Parmesan cheese, grated

Preheat the oven to 180°C/350°F/Gas mark 4.

Heat 2 tablespoons oil in a large frying pan over a medium heat.
Add the onion and cook for 5 minutes. Add the tomatoes and
garlic and simmer over a low heat for 10 minutes, stirring
frequently. Add the basil and seasoning and set aside.

Preheat the grill to high.

Brush the aubergine and courgettes with the remaining oil, and
place them on the grill. Add the pepper quarters to the grill,
skin-side up. Cook the peppers until the skin is charred, then
remove them from the grill and peel. Return the peppers to the
grill, cover and cook for 8 minutes. Remove the vegetables from
the grill and set aside.

Lightly oil a shallow baking dish. Spread a thin layer of the
tomato sauce in the bottom of the dish. Layer the vegetables,
then the Mozzarella, and the remaining tomato sauce, ending
with a layer of vegetables. Mix together the breadcrumbs and the
Parmesan in a small bowl and sprinkle on top.

Bake for 30 minutes, until the top is golden brown. Let stand for 10 minutes before serving.

ITALIAN OMELETTE

Serves 4

INGREDIENTS
6 sun-dried tomatoes
50ml/2fl oz olive oil
1 onion, finely chopped
1/2 tsp dried thyme
6 eggs
25g/1oz Parmesan cheese, grated
Salt and pepper

Place the tomatoes in a bowl and pour over enough hot water to cover. Leave to soak for 15 minutes, then lift out the tomatoes and pat dry with kitchen paper, reserving the soaking water. Cut the tomatoes into thin strips.

Heat the oil in a frying pan. Add the onion and cook for 5 minutes, then add the thyme and tomatoes and cook for a further 2 minutes.

Break the eggs into a bowl and beat lightly. Stir in 3 tablespoons of the tomato soaking water and the Parmesan and season to taste.

Add the eggs to the pan and mix quickly into the other ingredients. Lower the heat to medium and cook for 5 minutes, or until the base is golden.

Flip the omelette over and cook the other side for 4 minutes until golden brown. Remove the pan from the heat. Cut the omelette into wedges, garnish with thyme sprigs and serve immediately or leave to cool.

VEGETABLE KEBABS

Makes 32

INGREDIENTS
1 red pepper, chopped
1 green pepper, chopped
3 baby yellow squash, chopped
2 courgettes, cut into 2.5cm/1in slices
2 red onions, cut into wedges
225g/8oz tempeh, diced into 2.5cm/1in pieces
15 button mushrooms, quartered
250ml/9fl oz vegetable stock
2 garlic cloves, crushed
1 tsp grated fresh ginger
1 red chilli, seeded and chopped
1 tbsp tomato paste
Grated zest and juice of 1 lemon
Salt and pepper

Thread the vegetables and tempeh on to bamboo skewers, then place the kebabs into a large sealable container.

Combine the stock, garlic, ginger, chilli, tomato paste, lemon juice and zest and seasoning. Pour the marinade over the kebabs and leave to marinate overnight. Barbecue until well browned and cooked through, then serve.

TOFU AND VEGETABLES

Serves 2

INGREDIENTS
50ml/2fl oz orange juice
1/2 red chilli, seeded and finely chopped
1 tsp sesame oil
1 tbsp soy sauce
1 tbsp grated fresh ginger
250g/9oz tofu, cut into 2.5cm/1in cubes
1 tbsp sesame seeds
3 tbsp olive oil
4 spring onions, thinly sliced
275g/10oz mange tout
1/4 red pepper, finely sliced
1/4 green pepper, finely sliced
100g/4oz water chestnuts, sliced
25g/1oz fresh beanshoots

To make the dressing, combine the orange juice, chilli, sesame oil, soy sauce and ginger in a screw-top jar and shake vigorously. Place the tofu in a bowl and cover with the dressing. Leave to marinate for 20 minutes. Place the sesame seeds in a frying pan and dry toast for 30 seconds, then remove from the pan and set aside.

Heat half the oil in the frying pan over a medium heat. Remove the tofu from the dressing and place in the pan. Cook for 3 minutes or until golden, tossing regularly. Remove from the pan and place on kitchen paper.

Wipe the frying pan and return to a medium heat. Add the remaining oil and add the spring onion, mange tout and peppers. Cook for 2 minutes. Return the tofu to the pan, then add the water chestnuts and bean shoots. Add the dressing and toss gently. Cook for 2 minutes or until the tofu and vegetables are warmed through. Serve sprinkled with the toasted sesame seeds (optional).

BOK CHOI STIR-FRY

Serves 2

INGREDIENTS
50g/2oz wholemeal spaghetti
2 tbsp dry sherry
2 tbsp water
2 tbsp soy sauce
4 garlic cloves, crushed
5cm/2in piece fresh ginger , peeled and chopped
2 tsp olive oil
150g/5oz bok choi, sliced
100g/4oz shiitake mushrooms, sliced
3 spring onions, sliced
Salt and pepper

Bring a large saucepan of water to the boil. Add the spaghetti and boil for 5 minutes, or according to the packet instructions. Drain and set aside. Combine the sherry, water, soy sauce, garlic and ginger in a small bowl.

Heat the oil in a large frying pan. Add the spaghetti, bok choi and mushrooms and stir-fry for 2 minutes. Add the sauce and toss with the vegetables for a further 2 minutes. Add the spring onions and season to taste. Toss well and serve.

NUT AND CHEESE LOAF

Serves 6-8

INGREDIENTS
2 tbsp virgin olive oil, plus extra for greasing
2 onions
4 garlic cloves, crushed
2 celery stalks, finely sliced
175g/6oz cooked chestnuts, peeled
200g/7oz mixed nuts, chopped
50g/2oz fresh wholemeal breadcrumbs
225g/8oz Stilton cheese, crumbled
1 tbsp chopped fresh basil, plus extra sprigs to garnish
1 egg, beaten
Salt and pepper
1 courgette, cut into wedges
1 red pepper, skinned, cut into thin wedges

Preheat the oven to 180°C/350°F/Gas mark 4. Lightly grease a
900g/2lb loaf tin with oil.

Finely chop one of the onions. Heat 1 tablespoon oil in a frying
pan over a medium heat, add the chopped onion, 2 garlic cloves
and the celery and cook for 5 minutes, stirring occasionally.

Transfer the contents of the pan to a colander and drain well, then
transfer to a blender or food processor with the chestnuts, nuts,
breadcrumbs, half the cheese and the basil. Blend together, then
slowly add in the egg until a stiff mixture forms. Season to taste.

Cut the remaining onion into thin wedges. Heat the remaining oil
in a frying pan over a medium heat, add the onion, remaining
garlic, courgette and red pepper and cook for 5 minutes, stirring
frequently. Remove from the pan, season to taste and drain
through a colander.

Place half the nut mixture in the prepared loaf tin and smooth
the surface. Arrange the onion and pepper mixture on top and

crumble over the remaining cheese. Top with the remaining nut mixture and press down firmly. Cover with aluminium foil.

Bake in the oven for 45 minutes. Remove the foil and bake for a further 30 minutes, or until cooked and firm to the touch. Remove from the oven and leave to cool for 5 minutes before inverting on to a serving plate.

RATATOUILLE

Serves 8

INGREDIENTS
175ml/6fl oz olive oil
450g/1lb courgette, sliced
1 onion, sliced
400g/14oz aubergine, cut into 2.5cm/1in cubes
2 green peppers, sliced
3 garlic cloves, crushed
400g/14oz canned chopped tomatoes
1 tbsp dried oregano
100g/4oz canned stoned black olives, drained and sliced
Salt and pepper

Heat the oil in a frying pan over a medium heat. Add the courgette, onion, aubergine, peppers and garlic.

Sauté for 15 to 20 minutes, stirring occasionally. Add the tomatoes and their liquid, oregano, olives and seasoning.

Stir well, turn the heat down to low and let the whole thing simmer, covered for 40 minutes. Serve hot.

ROAST AUBERGINE WITH GOATS' CHEESE

Serves 6

INGREDIENTS
2 garlic cloves, crushed
1 tbsp fresh thyme leaves
3 tsp olive oil, divided
100g/4oz fresh goats' cheese
1 large aubergine
Salt and pepper
275g/10oz fresh spinach, washed and stems removed
2 small red peppers, roasted, peeled, seeded and diced
3 very ripe plum tomatoes, peeled, seeded, cored and diced
3 tbsp coarsely chopped fresh basil
Juice of 1 lemon

Mix half of the garlic, thyme, and 1 teaspoon oil in a large bowl.
Crumble the goats' cheese into the bowl, and toss lightly to
ensure the cheese is evenly coated. Cover and allow to sit at
room temperature for 30 minutes.

Lay the aubergine slices on a baking tray and sprinkle them with
salt. Allow them to sit for about 10 minutes.

Preheat the oven to 230°C/450°F/Gas mark 8.

Using kitchen paper, blot away the liquid released from the
aubergine and brush off the salt. Pat the skin dry. Brush both sides
of the aubergine with the remaining oil. Roast for about 5 minutes
or until the slices begin to colour slightly. Remove from the oven.
Heat the remaining oil in a large frying pan over a medium heat.
Add the remaining garlic and cook for 1 minute. Add the spinach
to the pan and season to taste. Cook over a medium heat for 2
minutes, covered. Remove from the heat and drain off the excess
water. Mix the spinach with the peppers in a medium-sized bowl.

In a small bowl, mix together the tomatoes, basil, lemon juice
and seasoning.

To serve, place an aubergine slice on each plate, with the spinach and pepper mixture spooned in the centre and another aubergine slice on top. Make another layer with the goats' cheese and then finally top with the tomato mixture.

FRITTATA

Serves 4

INGREDIENTS
15g/½oz butter, plus extra for greasing
6 mushrooms, sliced
2 leeks, sliced
1 red pepper, diced
1 aubergine, peeled and diced
1 courgette, diced
400g/14oz canned artichokes hearts, quartered
400g/14oz canned spinach, drained
8 eggs
225ml/8fl oz sour cream
150g/5oz Cheddar cheese, grated

Preheat the oven to 180°C/350°F/Gas mark 4. Lightly grease a baking dish with butter.

Heat the butter in a large saucepan and sauté the mushrooms and leeks for 3 minutes. Add pepper, aubergine and courgette and continue to stir-fry until cooked through.

Scatter the vegetables, artichokes and spinach in the prepared baking dish, and set aside.

In a mixing bowl, whisk the eggs until well beaten, add the sour cream and cheese, mix well, then pour over the vegetables. Bake in the oven for 40 minutes and serve in slices.

COURGETTE CASSEROLE

Serves 6

INGREDIENTS
25g/1oz butter, plus extra for greasing
650g/ 1lb 7oz courgettes, sliced
2 eggs, beaten
1 tbsp plain flour
1/2 tsp ground nutmeg
1/2 tsp dry mustard
2 tsp sugar substitute
Salt and pepper
225ml/8fl oz double cream
175g/6oz Cheddar cheese, grated

Preheat the oven to 170°C/325°F/Gas mark 3 and grease a large casserole dish with butter.

Melt the butter in a large frying pan. Add the courgettes and sauté over a medium-high heat until tender, stirring frequently. When done, remove from the heat and allow to cool slightly, then place in the prepared casserole dish.

Combine the eggs, flour, nutmeg, mustard, sugar substitute and seasoning to taste, in a large mixing bowl and mix together well. Stir in the cream and Cheddar.

Add the egg mixture to the courgettes and mix well. Place in the oven and bake for 30 minutes or until set. Cool and serve.

STUFFED AUBERGINES

Serves 4

INGREDIENTS
2 aubergines
Salt and pepper
2 tomatoes
1 garlic clove, crushed
1 onion, finely chopped
20 button mushrooms, sliced
200g/7oz cooked basmati rice
200g/7oz cooked chickpeas
4 tbsp finely chopped fresh basil leaves
1 tbsp finely chopped fresh rosemary
1 tbsp finely chopped fresh marjoram
1 tbsp lemon juice

Preheat the oven to 200°C/400°F/Gas mark 6.

Halve the aubergines lengthways. Scoop out the flesh leaving 1cm/1/2in of flesh inside the aubergine shells, reserving the flesh. Sprinkle the shells with salt and allow to stand for 20 minutes, then rinse and pat dry. Place the shells on a baking tray and bake in the oven for 15 minutes.

Meanwhile, sprinkle the aubergine flesh with salt, place in a colander in the sink and place a weighted plate on top, let stand for 2 hours before rinsing and patting dry. Chop the aubergine finely. Cut a cross into the bottom of each tomato and drop into boiling water for 30 seconds, then peel and dice.

Sauté the garlic and onion in a little water for 3 minutes. Add the mushrooms and a little more water and stir-fry for a further 3 minutes. Add the aubergine flesh, tomatoes, rice, chickpeas, herbs, lemon juice and seasoning. Cook for 6 minutes.

Spoon the mixture into the aubergine shells. Return to the oven for 15 minutes. Serve hot.

DESSERTS

Although desserts and sweet things are often banned on diets, the secret is more moderation, and picking desserts that fit in to the low-carb plan. Although many of these desserts feature fresh fruit – such as berry compote, baked bananas, fruit salad and raspberry parfait – there is also a little chocolate and a dash of fudge. The key is to look at the serving guide. If a dish says that it serves 4, then make sure you only eat a quarter of it – diets do not work if you eat more than the recommended amount!

CRÈME BRÛLÉE

Serves 4

INGREDIENTS
150g/5oz fresh blueberries
150g/5oz stoned fresh cherries
2 tbsp Cointreau
250g/9oz mascarpone cheese
200ml/7fl oz crème fraîche
3 tbsp dark muscovado sugar

Place the blueberries and cherries in the base of 4 150ml/1/4pt
ramekins. Sprinkle with Cointreau.

Cream the cheese in a mixing bowl until soft, then gradually beat
in the crème fraîche. Spoon the cheese mixture over the fruit,
then smooth the surface and ensure that the tops are level. Chill
in the refrigerator for at least 2 hours.

Sprinkle the tops with the sugar then, cook under a hot grill,
turning the dishes, for 3 to 4 minutes, or until the tops are lightly
caramelized. Serve immediately.

YOGURT PARFAITS

Serves 4

INGREDIENTS
150g/5oz muesli
200g/7oz fresh cherries
900ml/11/2pts vanilla yogurt

Divide the muesli evenly between 4 dessert dishes.

Arrange the cherries attractively on top of the muesli. Spoon the
yogurt over the top and serve immediately.

PEACH FROZEN YOGURT

Serves 4

INGREDIENTS
8 cardamom pods
500g/1lb 2oz peaches, stoned and chopped
2 tbsp water
200ml/7fl oz natural yogurt

Crush the cardamom pods with a pestle and mortar.

Place the peaches in a pan. Add the crushed cardamom pods and the water. Cover and simmer gently for 10 minutes. Remove the pan from the heat and leave to cool.

Tip the mixture into a blender or food processor and process until smooth, then press through a sieve placed over a bowl.

Add the yogurt to the purée and mix together. Pour into a plastic freezer-proof tub and freeze for about 6 hours until firm, beating once or twice to break up the ice crystals.

PEARS IN RED WINE

Serves 2

INGREDIENTS
1 tbsp grated lemon zest
1 cinnamon stick, crumbled
1 tbsp apple juice concentrate
125ml/4fl oz water
200ml/7fl oz red wine
2 Beurre Bosc pears
4 tbsp berry yogurt

Place the lemon zest in a medium-sized saucepan with the cinnamon, apple juice concentrate, water and red wine. Simmer over low heat, covered, for 5 minutes. Peel the pears and cut vertically into quarters, removing the core and seeds. Add the pears to the saucepan and simmer for 10 to 15 minutes, turning pears regularly and basting with syrup.

To serve, place the pear segments in a bowl, spoon the yogurt over and drizzle with the wine syrup.

COFFEE CAKE

Serves 12

INGREDIENTS
Butter, for greasing
225ml/8fl oz sour cream
150ml/¼pt olive oil
3 eggs
125ml/4fl oz water
2 tsp almond extract
100g/4oz whey powder
25g/1oz oat flour
2 tbsp vital wheat gluten
1 tsp baking soda
1 tbsp baking powder
2 tsp cinnamon
75g/3oz sugar substitute
50g/2oz chopped nuts
¼ tsp cinnamon

Preheat the oven to 180°C/350°F/Gas mark 4 and grease a springform tin with butter.

Combine the sour cream, oil, eggs, water and almond extract. Mix these ingredients together well.

Add the whey powder, oat flour, vital wheat gluten, baking soda, baking powder, cinnamon and 50g/2oz sugar substitute. Mix well and pour into the prepared tin.

Combine the remaining sugar substitute, nuts and cinnamon to make the topping and sprinkle it over the batter in the tin. Bake for 30 to 35 minutes. Leave to cool in the tin for 10 minutes, before turning out on to a wire rack to cool.

RASPBERRY PARFAIT

Serves 2

INGREDIENTS
100g/4oz fresh raspberries
$1/4$ tsp sugar substitute
225ml/8fl oz strawberry yogurt
1 tbsp chopped pecans, toasted

Purée the raspberries in a blender or food processor and add the sugar substitute.

Divide half the yogurt between two serving bowls or parfait glasses. Pour in half the puréed raspberries and top with the remaining yogurt. Pour the remaining sauce over the yogurt and top with the toasted pecans. Refrigerate until ready to serve.

CHOCOLATE FUDGE

Serves 40

INGREDIENTS
250ml/9fl oz double cream
225g/8oz unsweetened chocolate, broken into pieces
100g/4oz sugar substitute
25g/1oz butter
1 tbsp vanilla essence

Line a baking tray with greaseproof paper. Place a medium-size saucepan over a medium heat and add the cream. Bring to the boil, add the chocolate and stir until completely melted.

Remove the pan from the heat and add the sugar substitute, butter and vanilla essence. Mix until smooth and thoroughly combined. Transfer to the prepared baking sheet. Spread evenly over the entire sheet. Refrigerate until cool and stiff, about 2 hours. To serve, cut the fudge into squares.

BAKED BANANAS

← - ... ✓

Serves 6

INGREDIENTS
Vegetable oil, for greasing
100g/4oz sugar-free butter cookies, crumbled
2 tsp canola oil
1 tsp butter, melted
1 egg white
1 tsp lemon juice
2 tbsp clear honey
3 bananas

Preheat the oven to 230°C/450°F/Gas mark 8. Line a baking tray
with aluminium foil, then set a baking rack on top and brush it
with vegetable oil.

In a shallow dish, combine the cookie crumbs, canola oil and
butter. Mix until well blended and set aside.

In a medium-sized bowl, whisk together the egg white, lemon
juice and honey, then set aside.

Peel the bananas and trim the pointed tips. Cut the bananas
crosswise into 2cm/³⁄₄in pieces. Dip each banana piece into the
egg white mixture, then transfer them to the crumb mixture. Roll
the banana pieces in the crumbs to coat them. Place the bananas
on the prepared baking rack.

Bake the bananas for about 10 minutes and serve hot.

BERRY COMPOTE

Serves 6

INGREDIENTS
300g/11oz assorted frozen berries, thawed
2 tbsp water
1/4 tsp sugar substitute
75g/3oz butter

Simmer the berries with water in a medium-sized saucepan for about 5 minutes. Add the sugar substitute and butter and stir well to combine.

Remove the pan from the heat, stir, and divide the compote between 6 serving bowls.

FRUIT SALAD

Serves 4

INGREDIENTS
1 lime
1 pink grapefruit, peeled and segmented
2 oranges, peeled and segmented
4 apricots, diced
2 pears, cored and diced
2 apples, peeled, cored and diced
Juice of 1 orange
1 tsp cinnamon

Place all the ingredients in a large mixing bowl and toss together well. Place in a covered container and refrigerate for at least 12 hours before serving.

FUDGE CAKE

Serves 2

INGREDIENTS
50g/2oz plain chocolate
1 tbsp strong, decaffeinated black coffee
1/2 tsp sugar substitute
4 egg whites

Preheat the oven to 180°C/350°F/Gas mark 4.

Place the chocolate in a bowl and microwave on high for 2 minutes to melt or place in a bowl over a pan of simmering water. Stir in the coffee and sweetener.

Beat the egg whites until stiff peaks form, then fold into the chocolate mixture. Spoon into two small soufflé dishes and bake in the oven for 8 minutes. Serve warm.

RASPBERRY FOOL

Serves 4

INGREDIENTS
200ml/7fl oz light evaporated milk
1 tbsp caster sugar
450g/1lb fresh raspberries
Flesh of 2 passion fruit

In a large bowl, whip the evaporated milk and sugar together until the mixture is thick.

Purée the raspberries in a blender or food processor, reserving a few for garnish, then stir into the whipped evaporated milk with the passion fruit. Spoon into serving dishes and serve decorated with the reserved raspberries.

SNACKS
&
DIPS

Snacking between meals is dangerous if you are trying to lose weight, but if you are going to indulge, then these low-carb snacks can cut the guilt factor in half. Some of them could even make great light lunches or party food, as well as sauces and dips to go with a salad. Dips include guacamole and coleslaw, while snacks range from French toast to devilled eggs and chicken wings. As long as you stick to the correct portion sizes then you shouldn't go far wrong!

HUMMUS

Makes 450g/1lb

INGREDIENTS
400g/14oz canned chickpeas, drained
2 tbsp tahini paste
5 tbsp virgin olive oil
5 tbsp lemon juice
3 garlic cloves, crushed
2 tbsp hot water
Salt and pepper

Put the first 5 ingredients into a blender or food processor and blend to form a smooth paste. Slowly blend in the hot water and season to taste.

Spoon into a serving dish, cover and store in the refrigerator until required.

PESTO SCRAMBLED EGGS

Serves 2

INGREDIENTS
150g/5oz salad leaves
225ml/8fl oz egg substitute
2 tsp prepared pesto
2 tsp olive oil
2 tbsp grated Parmesan cheese

Place the lettuce in a microwave-safe bowl and microwave on high for 3 minutes. Place on 2 plates. Mix the egg substitute and pesto together. Heat the oil in a medium-sized non-stick frying pan over a high heat. Reduce the heat to low, or remove the pan from the heat, and add the egg mixture. Scramble for about 1 minute, or until set to desired consistency. Place over the lettuce and sprinkle with Parmesan cheese.

In a large mixing bowl, whisk together the mayonnaise, mustard, sugar substitute and vinegar.

Add the cabbage, onion, carrot and seasoning, and mix well to coat. Refrigerate for at least 1 hour before serving.

DOLMADES

Makes 30

INGREDIENTS
30 vine leaves
175g/6oz basmati rice
2 tbsp lemon juice
500ml/16fl oz water
Salt and pepper

Preheat the oven to 180°C/350°F/Gas mark 4.

Boil the rice until nearly cooked, then drain and set aside to cool.

In a bowl combine the rice, lemon juice and seasoning. In a colander, separate the vine leaves, and rinse to drain off excess brine.

On a flat surface, place each vine leaf shiny-side down. Place a small amount of the rice mixture in the middle of each leaf. Fold in each side and carefully roll up.

When all the rice has been used, place the dolmades in a bowl side by side. Place a weight on top to prevent them unravelling, then pour 450ml/³/₄pt of cold water over. Cook in the oven for 10 minutes, or until vine leaves are soft.

CHEESE STICKS

Makes 8 servings

INGREDIENTS
175g/6oz ground pork rinds
2¹/₂ tbsp soy protein isolate
¹/₄ tsp lemon pepper
1 tsp Italian seasoning
1 egg
1 tbsp water
225g/8oz Mozzarella, cut into 16 sticks
50g/2oz lard

Combine the pork rinds, soy protein isolate, lemon pepper and Italian seasoning in a shallow dish. In a separate dish, combine the egg and water. Melt the lard in a medium-sized frying pan over medium heat.

Dip the cheese sticks into the egg mixture, then into the pork rind mixture. Fry them over a medium heat until brown. Serve warm.

DEVILLED EGGS

Serves 6

INGREDIENTS
6 hard-boiled eggs
2 tsp Dijon mustard
75ml/3fl oz mayonnaise
¹/₄ tsp salt

Slice the eggs in half and carefully remove the yolks into a mixing bowl.

Mash the yolks with a fork. Stir in the mustard, mayonnaise and salt and mix until creamy. Spoon the mixture back into the egg whites.

MAYONNAISE

Makes 225ml/8fl oz

INGREDIENTS
1 egg yolk
1 tsp salt
1/2 tsp Tabasco sauce
1 tsp dry mustard
11/2 tbsp vinegar
11/2 tbsp lemon juice
150ml/1/4pt olive vegetable oil

Place the egg yolk, salt, Tabasco sauce, mustard, vinegar and
lemon juice in a blender or food processor.

With the blender running, pour in the oil in a thin stream. The
mayonnaise will start to thicken. When it gets thick enough that
oil starts to collect on top, stop adding oil and turn off the blender.

Store in a tightly covered jar in the refrigerator.

CHICKEN WINGS

Makes 25

INGREDIENTS
450g/1lb chicken wings
75g/3oz Parmesan cheese, grated
1 tbsp dried parsley
1 tsp paprika
1 tsp dried oregano
Salt and pepper
50g/2oz butter

Preheat the oven to 180°C/350°F/Gas mark 4.

Cut the wings into drumsticks.

Combine the Parmesan, parsley, paprika, oregano and seasoning in a bowl. Line a shallow baking tin with aluminium foil.

Melt the butter in a shallow pan. Dip each drumstick in the butter, then roll in the cheese and seasoning mixture and arrange in the foil-lined tin and bake in the oven for 1 hour.

COLESLAW

Serves 10

INGREDIENTS
450ml/3/4pt mayonnaise
1¹/₂ tsp dry mustard
4 tsp sugar substitute
4 tbsp white wine vinegar
250g/9oz red cabbage, shredded
1 onion, diced
1 carrot, grated
Salt and pepper

GUACAMOLE

Serves 1

INGREDIENTS
1 avocado
Juice of 1/2 lime
1 tbsp finely chopped onion
1/2 garlic clove, finely chopped
1 tomato, diced
1 tbsp chopped fresh coriander leaves
1/2 tsp finely chopped red chilli
Pinch of mild chilli powder
Pinch of cumin powder

Cut the avocado in half and scoop out the flesh. Roughly mash the flesh with a fork and stir in the lime juice.

Add the onion, garlic, tomato, coriander and chilli pepper, mix them in well and season with chilli powder and cumin.

CHEESE OMELETTE

Serves 1

INGREDIENTS
15g/1/2oz butter
2 eggs, beaten
75g/3oz Cheddar cheese, grated

Heat the butter in a frying pan over a medium-high heat. Pour in the eggs, they should immediately start to set.

When the bottom layer of egg is set around the edges, lift the edge using a spatula and tip the pan to let the raw egg flow underneath. Do this all around the edges.

Turn the heat down to low and place the cheese on one half of the omelette, cover the pan with a lid and let it sit over very low heat for a minute or two.

When your omelette is done, slip a spatula under the half without the filling, fold it over and then lift the whole thing on to a plate.

FRENCH TOAST

Serves 6

INGREDIENTS
125ml/4fl oz double cream
4 eggs
125ml/4fl oz water
1 tsp vanilla essence
6 slices low-carb wholewheat bread
Butter, for frying

Beat together the cream, eggs, water and vanilla extract and place the mixture in a shallow dish, such as a pie plate.

Soak each slice of bread in the mixture for at least 5 minutes, turning once.

Fry each piece of bread in plenty of butter over a medium heat. Brown well on each side and serve immediately.

STUFFED EGGS

Serves 4

INGREDIENTS
1 tsp canola oil
1/2 tsp butter
2 shallots, finely chopped
150g/5oz button mushrooms, finely chopped
Juice of 1 lemon
1 tsp finely grated lemon zest
Salt and pepper
5 hard-boiled eggs, peeled
3 tbsp mayonnaise
50g/2oz Gruyere cheese, grated
Pinch of cayenne pepper

Warm the oil and butter in a frying pan over a medium heat. Add the shallots and cook for 3 minutes, until soft. Stir in the mushrooms, lemon juice and lemon zest. Season to taste. Cover and cook, stirring frequently, for 10 minutes, or until the liquid has evaporated. Remove from heat.

Preheat the oven to 190°C/375°F/Gas mark 5.

Slice 4 of the hard-boiled eggs lengthways. Remove the yolks and carefully slice a small piece from the bottom of each egg white half so that it will stand flat and steady on a platter.

Chop the remaining egg and the yolks and press it through a fine-mesh sieve into the pan with the mushrooms. Stir in the mayonnaise and add 2 tablespoons of the cheese and the cayenne.

Place an equal portion of the mushroom mixture in each egg-white half. Place the filled egg halves in a baking dish and sprinkle the tops with the remaining cheese and bake for 4 minutes, then cook under a low grill for about 2 minutes, until golden brown. Serve hot.

BEETROOT DIP

Serves 20

INGREDIENTS
4 beetroots
150g/5oz cottage cheese
100g/4oz low-fat natural yogurt
2 tbsp lime juice
Salt and pepper

Preheat oven to 220°C/425°F/Gas mark 7.

Slice beetroot in half, place on aluminium foil squares and tightly wrap, then place on a baking tray and bake in the oven for 30 minutes or until cooked. Remove the beetroot from the foil and place in a blender or food processor.

Add the remaining ingredients and blend well. Season to taste and serve.

PEANUT BUTTER COOKIES

Makes about 50

INGREDIENTS
100g/4oz butter, plus extra for greasing
100g/4oz sugar substitute
1 tbsp dark treacle
225g/8oz smooth peanut butter
1 egg
1/2 tsp salt
1/2 tsp baking soda
1/2 tsp vanilla essence
100g/4oz soya powder
2 tbsp oat bran

Preheat the oven to 190°C/375°F/Gas mark 5. Grease several baking trays with butter.

Use an electric mixer to beat the butter until creamy. Add the sugar substitute, treacle and beat again until well combined.

Beat in the peanut butter, egg, salt, baking soda and vanilla. Beat in the soya powder and oat bran.

Roll the dough into small balls and place them on the sheets, then press flat with the back of a fork. Bake in the oven for 10 to 12 minutes.

Allow to cool on a wire rack before serving.

CHEESE PUFFS

Serves 10

INGREDIENTS
75g/3oz cream cheese
100g/4oz Cheddar cheese, grated
100g/4oz butter
2 egg whites
1/4 tsp cream of tartar
100g/4oz plain pork rinds

Melt cream cheese, cheddar cheese and butter in a microwave or in a bowl over a pan of simmering water. Leave to cool for 5 minutes.

Meanwhile beat the egg whites with the cream of tartar until stiff. Carefully fold the cheese mixture into the egg whites. Dip the pork rinds into mixture to evenly coat and then place on greaseproof paper. Let stand in refrigerator overnight.

Preheat the oven to 130°C/250°F/Gas mark 1/2.

Spread the puffs evenly across a baking tray and bake for 1 hour, or until crisp.

BLACKBERRY SMOOTHIE

Serves 2

INGREDIENTS
2 bananas
300ml/1/2pt low-fat natural yogurt
400ml/14fl oz skimmed milk
1/2 tsp vanilla essence
150g/5oz blackberries

Place the yogurt, milk, bananas, vanilla essence and blackberries in a blender or food processor and purée until smooth. Serve in a tall glass.

PORRIDGE

Serves 2

INGREDIENTS
50g/2oz porridge oats
1 tbsp oatmeal
300ml/1/2pt skimmed milk
25g/1oz sultanas
1 banana, sliced
2 tsp clear honey
1 tsp flaked almonds

Place the oats, oatmeal and milk in a saucepan and cook over a medium heat for 5 minutes, stirring continuously.

Transfer to 2 serving bowls, add the sultanas and banana and spoon the honey over. Sprinkle with the almonds and serve.

CHILLI COLESLAW

Serves 6

1 red chilli, seeded and chopped
2 garlic cloves, crushed
100g/4oz fresh coriander leaves, chopped
2 tbsp chopped fresh mint leaves
Grated zest and juice of 1 lime
4 tbsp olive oil
4 tbsp sour cream
Salt and pepper
1 green cabbage, chopped
1 red onion, sliced

Combine the chilli, garlic, coriander, mint, lime zest and juice, olive oil, sour cream and seasoning to taste in a blender or food processor.

Place in covered container in refrigerator and leave overnight. Combine the cabbage and onion, then mix through the dressing and serve.

MARSHMALLOWS

Serves 8

INGREDIENTS
75g/3oz cornflour
150g/5oz caster sugar
2 tsp unflavored gelatine
75ml/3fl oz water
100g/4oz granulated sugar
125ml/4fl oz corn syrup
1/4 tsp salt
1 tsp vanilla essence

Sift together the cornflour and caster sugar. Lightly grease a 20cm/8in baking tin with butter and sprinkle with 1 tablespoon of the cornflour mixture. Tilt the tin to coat

Blend the gelatine and water in a small saucepan and allow to soak. Add the granulated sugar and stir over a low heat until the gelatine and sugar are dissolved.

In a blender or food processor, combine the gelatine mixture, corn syrup, salt and vanilla. Beat until peaks form. Spread the gelatin mixture over the bottom of the prepared tin and smooth the top. Let stand for 2 hours or until well set.

With a wet knife, cut the marshmallow mixture into quarters and loosen around the edges. Sprinkle remaining cornstarch on a baking tray and invert the marshmallows onto it. Cut each quarter into 9 pieces and roll in the cornflour mixture. Place the marshmallows on a rack and cover with kitchen paper. Let stand overnight before serving.

LEEK CAKES

Serves 4

INGREDIENTS
2 eggs
300ml/1/2pt milk
250g/9oz brown rice flour
Salt and pepper
300g/11oz leeks, chopped
3 tbsp olive oil

Finely chop the leeks in a blender or food processor.

Mix together the eggs, milk, flour and seasoning to form a batter, then add the leeks and mix well.

Heat the oil in a frying pan until hot, then cook the batter like pancakes. Serve hot.